"Most people struggle with the fear of rejection at some time in their lives. Gail Porter offers encouragement by sharing her own honest story and the inspiring stories of others. The division of sections in *Will the Real Person Please Stand Up?* provides a brilliant summary of her book: living in captivity, breaking strongholds, and tasting freedom. Gail nailed it when she explained that we wear masks because we think we're not good enough, need to be perfect, or must measure up to a perceived standard. Many will relate to living in isolation rather than taking the risk of being their authentic selves. She reminds us that the One who matters most has loved us all along, faults included. I have no doubt Gail's writings will inspire many to rise above the fear of rejection and live the life of freedom God intended. As a bonus, she has included study questions at the end of each chapter. They will make this book easy to use in a small-group setting."

DENA YOHE
Co-founder of Hope for Hurting Parents
Award-winning author of *You Are Not Alone*
Coordinator of Prayer for Prodigals (a ministry of Cru)

"In four-plus decades of speaking and counseling, I've consistently heard one word. That word is 'authentic.' As you begin this book, you will see and feel authenticity—not just in its words, but in its author, Gail Porter. Gail is a friend and a fellow traveler in our journey to find meaning, purpose, and fulfillment in our day-to-day lives. This book is both honest and emotionally engaging because it comes from Gail's heart, a heart that is open, caring, and yes—authentic."

JIM KELLER
Founder, Charis Counseling Center
Orlando, Florida

"The world waits for the 'real you' to emerge and rise up to fulfill your God-given destiny and purpose. Gail has brilliantly given us the master plan. Read it, live it, see it change your life."

SCOTT GEORGE
Senior Pastor, Pine Castle United Methodist Church and
Orlando Hope Executive Team

"Fear paralyzes. In the book *Will the Real Person Please Stand Up?*, author Gail Porter describes how fear of rejection layers our hearts and robs us of many blessings. Based on her own lifelong struggle with an irrational, fear-based identity, Gail shares ways to break the strongholds that take us captive. She also teaches her readers how to embrace the present without encumbrances of the past. Her practical, action-based steps give us new determination to climb mountains, so we can anticipate our futures with joy."

JEANNE LeMAY
Award-winning author of
Dear God I'm Desperate: Women Have Issues, God Has Answers
www.jeannelemay.com

"Gail Porter's use of personal stories invites you to feel your own pain. She then gives hope as she beautifully showcases, 'up close and personal,' God's healing of the fear of rejection."

LOTTIE K. HILLARD, LMHC

"In *Will the Real Person Please Stand Up?*, Gail succinctly unveils what imprisons and inhibits many of us: the inability to express our authentic selves. With honesty and openness, Gail reveals this effective ploy of the enemy. He deceives us into believing we need to please others to be loved, build walls to stay safe and pain free, and prevent others from knowing and rejecting the real us. No more! In this most enlightening, encouraging, and inspiring book, Gail provides Bible-based solutions for recognizing, confronting, and conquering our fear. Now we can live victoriously, be all we can be, and experience everything our Creator has in store for us. It is time to *Stand Up*! Thank you, Gail!"

MARVIN R. TERRY, DC
Whole Health Alternatives

Will the REAL PERSON Please Stand Up?

WILL THE REAL PERSON PLEASE STAND UP?
By Gail Porter

PUBLISHED BY REDEMPTION PRESS
PO Box 427 Enumclaw, WA 98022

ISBN- 978-1-68314-689-6 (Softcover)
ISBN- 978-1-68314-690-2 (Epub)
ISBN- 978-1-68314-691-9 (Mobi)

Cover design by Bill Johnson
Book design by CJ Wright

Printed in the United States of America

Will the REAL PERSON Please Stand Up?

GAIL PORTER

I dedicate this book
to my longtime friend Shirley Mewhinney.

Thank you for traveling with me on this amazing journey of discovery.
Your prayers, encouragement, insights, advice, humor,
and willingness to speak the truth in love
have given me courage to step forward and taste freedom
to become the real me.

Acknowledgments

To my writer friends in the Orlando Chapter of Word Weavers International. You gave me courage to become a serious writer and joined me in this journey of learning to communicate effectively with readers. Your friendships welcomed me into the Orlando writing community and paved the way for me to step into other opportunities as well.

To Enid, Connie, Margie, Janice, Kim, Sharon, Shirley, Brent, and Jo. Thank you for your willingness to share your deep and personal stories. You showed readers they are not alone and helped them embrace hope for rising above their fear of rejection.

To my encouragers at PCUMC. I am blessed by your personal interest in my life. Thank you for coming alongside me as I partnered with God to write about this difficult topic while trusting Him to bring about life change. You stood with me, instilling confidence, praying for specific needs, and cheering me on by saying, "You can do this."

To other personal friends in different arenas of life. Thank you for your cherished friendship and your spiritual encouragement. They help me stay strong as a woman of God who desires to help others know God and live for Him.

To the team at Redemption Press. Thank you, team, and special thanks to Christina Miller. Your expert coaching and editing helped us create the best book this could be. Thank you for your affirmation and encouragement that strengthened me throughout this journey.

To my Father God, Shepherd Jesus, and my Holy Spirit Counselor and Companion, who stayed by my side throughout this project, giving me wisdom to write the words God wanted to say to those who desire to be set free.

Do not call to mind the former things,
Or ponder things of the past.
Behold, I will do something new,
Now it will spring forth;
Will you not be aware of it?
I will even make a roadway in the wilderness,
Rivers in the desert.

Isaiah 43:18–19

Will The Real Person Please Stand Up?
Contents

Reflection Questions at the end of each chapter.
Journal Your Journey section at the back of the book.

Introduction

An Invitation to a Journey toward Freedom

I didn't want to delve below the surface. I was afraid of what I'd find.

Living a superficial life seemed easier. Driven by a need for love and acceptance, I stayed in hiding and presented myself as the person I thought everyone wanted me to be. In my mind, that way of life provided the best protection against my greatest fear: rejection.

The superficial life, however, robbed me of the joy of living in freedom. God wanted to set me free to become the person He created me to be.

Deep-sea diving is challenging, and many of us fear it because it takes us below the surface of safety. There, danger can arise when sharks, with the capability of killing us or maiming us for life, charge toward us. Likewise, living below the surface of our conscious thoughts can feel as dangerous as scuba diving because the enemy of our souls has the same capability of killing our joy of living.

Below the surface, though, we have the chance to observe the wonder of the sea creatures God created. In those same waters, away from the net of daily life, we can discover the beauty of God's creation of us.

Diving into those azure waters can help us uncover our fears. Realizing and acknowledging those fears can lead to the thrill of bursting from the depths into the freedom of the air above.

Are you aware of fears that keep you from experiencing freedom? Have you struggled with the same fear I have: rejection? Has that fear held you back from saying yes to wonderful opportunities and walking through open doors God has placed before you? You knew if you took the risk, your world could expand. Yet you said no.

God has plans and dreams for you. In His love, compassion, and grace, He will reveal the emotions and fears your experiences have formed. You can ask Him to release you from these emotions and fears. He is more powerful than all your hurts, wounds, disappointments, and fears. He can overcome everything that hinders you, so you can walk in freedom as the person He created you to be—the real you.

God helped me dive below the surface of my life. Once I uncovered my fear of rejection and released it to God, I could remove my facade and begin trusting His protection. I want to tell you about who I've become—the real me.

You will read about my experiences and the stories from others at various stages in their journeys toward freedom. The input from experts, also included, can help you better understand the fear of rejection and learn crucial ways to overcome its power.

Until you know you are under the influence of something or someone, you remain a victim. "Living in Captivity," the first section of this book, will show you how childhood patterns and experiences may have led you to devise techniques and strategies for the Great Cover-Up (my term). This cover-up prevented you from revealing your real self, uniquely and lovingly designed by God.

Once you realize the reasons for your captivity, then what? The second section, "Breaking Strongholds," presents action steps you can take to break the vicious cycle of isolation. My life began to change when I no longer wanted to exist as the person everyone else wanted me to be.

As you allow God to lead you out of captivity and break strongholds, you can begin "Tasting Freedom." In this third section, you will learn to embrace the present without being encumbered by the past. You'll begin to climb mountains with new determination and less fear, enjoy the view along the way, anticipate the future with joy, and live in freedom.

Psychiatrist Gail Saltz says in her book *Becoming Real*:

> Being real means experiencing life's gifts to their fullest. It means being authentic, strong, rooted. It means that along with the pains of loss, we get to experience the joys of closeness, connection, and intimacy. When we're real, we're no longer like tumbleweeds blown around where the wind blows. We have the strength, the stamina, the courage, the power, and the freedom to go where we want to go. Being real means we can tolerate life's discomforts and ambiguities because we are strong enough to embrace the good and the bad, the black, white, and grays of most situations. When we accept this truth, we will become like trees with deep roots—strong and capable and able to weather whatever comes our way. Being real means experiencing the full spectrum of human emotions.[1]

Where are you on your journey of discovering and acknowledging your fears and living in freedom?

In God's strength, people who struggle with the fear of rejection can walk out of their self-made prisons and taste the freedom that will allow them to become who God made them to be.

Come on a journey of discovering how to live in freedom, and become the real person God intended you to be all along.

Part One
Living in Captivity

Chapter 1
Seeking Love and Acceptance

M y mother and father didn't abuse me verbally, physically, or sexually. They didn't shout at me or use violence. They were good people who took care of my daily physical needs.

So why did I grow up feeling sad and lonely? Why did I feel disconnected and worthless? Why didn't I bond with anyone?

Because the nice people who raised me were empty.

Henri Nouwen, author and priest, describes how that feels:

> There is nothing so harmful as a relationship where nothing is given, nothing is asked, nothing is expected. This is the barren landscape where children grow up in a family where drawbridges are perennially up. This is the place where love is not expressed. Where there is no engagement. No openness. No participation. No joining. No common celebration. No ability to weep together. It is the place where there are no questions and therefore no answers. This place lacks passion and therefore lacks humanity. There are no easy formulas for receiving healing from such neglect.[2]

These words perfectly represent life within my family. Or perhaps I should say lack of life. Our home was a place of nothingness.

Psychotherapist Lottie Hillard says this kind of family dynamics exemplifies "benign neglect" and "a nice version of rejection."

My mother and father were kind and good people, but they disregarded the most important ingredients for our family: love and connection.

I never realized that truth before. I minimized my feelings and remained detached, never comprehending what was missing in our family.

As an adult, I tried to recall where my parents and my brother and I sat at our dining room table. I couldn't picture us together there. I didn't remember anything we talked about.

Someone asked me, "Why do you need to know? What does it matter?"

Not being able to picture the four of us during what would normally have been "family time" made me feel sad, lonely, unimportant, and unloved.

Now I grasp why I couldn't remember anything: nothing happened. I had no memories to latch on to because we weren't connected with love that would have fostered personal and meaningful conversations, smiles, and laughter.

There's no picture in my memory of my parents hugging and kissing me. They may have, but their hugs and kisses didn't leave an imprint on my heart.

I can't remember a gleam in their eyes when I bounced into the kitchen in the mornings or ran in from playing outside. I never heard, "That's wonderful" or "You're wonderful" when I told them something I'd said or done. Their lack of love and passion toward me made me feel I wasn't worth caring for. As a result, I stayed aloof and didn't bond with them.

Homesickness was never a problem for me, even during my elementary-school years, when I spent one week away at the annual Campfire Girls camp. During the four years I lived on my college campus, I seldom called, and I went home only on holidays and vacations. Even while working overseas for many years, I didn't experience a sense of missing out. The fact is, I wasn't.

I remember two conversations with Mom that could have elicited a response of encouragement from her, but they didn't. As a teenager, I told her I planned to submit a personal story to the humor section of *Reader's Digest* magazine. She said, "They may not think your story's funny and won't accept it." Instead of trying anyway, I never submitted it.

Toward the end of my junior year in college, I was elected sorority president. When I relayed the news to my mother, instead of congratulating me, she responded, "That's a lot of responsibility." Behind her words I heard this message: "I'm not sure you're capable. What if you fail?"

My parents divorced when I was fourteen and going into high school. My brother was a year ahead of me.

Dad and I saw each other from time to time. Five years later, when he married Connie, they welcomed me into their home and lives. Their love and acceptance paved the way for Dad and me to build a close relationship we relished for the rest of his years.

Dad's absence relieved some of the underlying tension in the house caused by frustration in their marriage. Because Mom had to deal with every detail of our daily lives while working full time, she didn't have time or energy left for Greig and me. The disconnection between the three of us widened.

Now I understand that my fear of rejection grew out of my lack of love from and connection with my parents, especially my mother.

Life coach Adam Sicinski sheds light on possible origins of fear of rejection:

You were not born with the fear of rejection. It is not a natural part of the human psyche . . . The primary reason [for the fear of rejection] is often a lack of self-esteem . . . Often low self-esteem stems back to childhood experience. Certain events might have taken place that made you doubt your own personal sense of worth. It could even have been one significant traumatic experience of rejection that changed everything. As a result, you became insecure and lacked the necessary belief in yourself that would help you to create your own identity in this world. [3]

Dr. Saltz says:

Since we are almost never told the truth—that living life brings inevitable pain—we think that each time we experience pain it is proof something's wrong with us. . . . Being human, we look to avoid pain, but when we do, we lose the opportunity to follow the pain to the deepest part of our unconscious minds where our stories sit, spinning their magic about what does and doesn't make us lovable, adequate, or acceptable. But it's only when we make the decision to go into these deep places that we reap the reward of breaking free from the old, restricting narratives we have long outgrown. [4]

Dynamics in our extended family impacted me as well. My Aunt Elia, eleven years younger than Mom, breezed in and out of my life during my early years. I liked her makeup and wavy brown hair and admired her life as a sophisticated single professional woman.

I enjoyed her visits, but even when we hadn't seen each other for a while, she didn't hug me or say, "I'm glad to see you." If she had, I would have tucked those hugs and words into my heart.

Through the years, she criticized more than praised. Determined that I would walk correctly, sit correctly, and use good grammar in my speech and writing, she often pointed out my errors. Sometimes that caused me to doubt her love.

One of her sons recently told me, "Mom loved you deeply. She talked about you all the time. You were the daughter she never had. The reason I wanted to stay connected with you after our mothers died is because I knew how Mom felt about you."

His tender words helped me realize I had misunderstood his mother. Aunt Elia did love me, but she didn't know how to show love. She corrected me out of a desire to help, yet I viewed her remarks as a sign that I was unlovable and unacceptable. In reality, my interpretation of her words stemmed from the message of rejection I'd already received from my parents.

The only person who never rejected me was my grandmother, affectionately called Grandmartie. She gave me continual hugs, endearing looks, encouraging words, and a sense of love that became my lifeline until her death, just short of age one hundred.

I remember Grandmartie pouring love and acceptance into my heart. One day she picked me up and laid me across her lap, wrapping her soft arms around my small body. I can still hear the melodious lullaby she sang over me as we swayed back and forth in the padded rocking chair in her den. Perhaps she cherished that tender moment as much as I do today.

Grandmartie's genuine love filled some empty spaces. Yet without receiving this kind of love and sense of belonging from my parents, I still floundered.

I didn't feel capable of establishing my own identity or my own voice within my family, and that lack of confidence stifled my emotions. If I felt hurt or disappointed by someone's comment or action, I didn't reveal that anything was wrong. Convinced it was less risky to pretend than to be honest, I stuffed my feelings inside and said nothing. My goal was simply to comply and hope they would accept me.

Dr. Saltz says, "When self-expression is blocked, we learn to pretend (to ourselves and to others) to be somebody else. Seeking approval, we migrate from who we really are to who we think our parents or teachers or grandparents want us to be. We adopt their expectations for who we should be."[5]

The lack of love and acceptance from my parents caused me to perform—as a child and even as an adult—to win people's acceptance.

Following my college graduation, I moved to California and began working and leading an independent life. While preparing for Mom's first visit, I noticed a shift in my view of our relationship.

I felt less guarded and more carefree as I made plans and pictured us talking about personal things and doing activities together. God gave me courage and desire to create space in my heart to love her in a new way. She would always be my mother, but I wanted to confide in her as I would a best friend.

When I saw her at the airport, I smiled and hugged her. "I feel as if I'm welcoming a friend!" I said.

She smiled, uncertain how to respond to my spontaneous comment.

We built wonderful memories during our visit. Mom seemed relaxed around me and more comfortable talking about personal things.

Later, during my years of living and working in the Philippines, she flew across the ocean three times to visit me, mostly at her initiation. On my first furlough to the US, she met me with a hug. Then she slipped her arm around my waist and kept it there as we walked arm in arm from the arrival area (permitted in those days) to the front of the airport. Those gestures of love continued during the rest of my furloughs before Mom died.

Relationships in our families determine how we respond, either positively or negatively, to people and to life. Our relationships and interaction with people outside our families can alter our lives as well, depending on whether we receive admiration or rejection.

My friend Enid engages with people easily, speaks to groups with confidence, and attracts admiration from everyone who meets her. I never thought she would struggle with the fear of rejection.

Recently we set a date for girl talk at a favorite restaurant. After submitting our order and exchanging family pictures, Enid asked, "How's your book project coming along?"

"Making a lot of progress. Since fear of rejection is so common, it's been easy to collect stories."

Enid looked down and ran her finger over the rim of her coffee cup. "Let me tell you my rejection story. I've begun to realize I fear that people will suddenly not want to be with me."

"I'm so surprised, Enid." I leaned closer and caught the shimmer in her eyes. "It's hard to imagine anyone not wanting to be your friend."

"Recently, a repressed memory came to me," she said. "It happened in kindergarten. I had two special friends in my class. We always played together during recess and even before class began.

"One morning when I arrived at the classroom, the two of them were already playing together in the corner. When I ran over to them, one girl said, 'We're both sick, so you can't play with us.' I knew they couldn't be sick or they wouldn't be at school. I realized they were telling me they no longer wanted to be friends with me.

"I started crying. My teacher came over to find out what was wrong. When I told her, she turned to other students in the room and said, 'Who wants to play with Enid?' I was afraid no one would. But Andrew said, 'I want to.' Andrew became my rescuer that day."

"How sad, Enid. Do you think this is when your fear started?"

"I think so, but more happened later. At my elementary school, I was the only black child in my class. Soon a white classmate and I became best friends. We had several of the same classes and always ate lunch together in the cafeteria. Soon she asked her mother if she could invite me home. Her mother discovered I was a black girl.

"The next day, my friend said, 'My mother won't let me be friends with you anymore.' Our friendship ended that day."

I couldn't imagine how Enid felt in that moment. All I could think to say was, "I'm so sorry that happened to you."

"Something else took place in college. Tyrone and I met in biology class, and eventually he became my boyfriend. During Christmas break, we both went home. I thought he would call me, but he didn't." When she looked up at me, pain still lingered in her eyes, after all these years.

"When I returned to campus and saw him, he admitted he had gotten back together with his old girlfriend. Another rejection. I was heartbroken."

I reached across the table and placed my hand on hers. "Such painful times. Do you still experience that fear?"

"I still have lingering questions. Will people welcome me? At times I feel the same emotion as I did during my school days."

Experiences like Enid's provide powerful examples of how the fear of rejection can stem from rejection by people outside our homes. Especially when those experiences happen at a young age, they can impact our thoughts, responses, and behavior into adulthood.

If we do not receive love and acceptance from our family and friends, that deficiency can affect the way we live, causing us to change in an attempt to win love, acceptance, and approval.

God knows that not all of us will feel loved and accepted in our families or by our friends. When we seek love and acceptance and can't find it, we believe something is wrong with us. We can become consumed with fear that others will not like our performance. This kind of focus prevents God's love from infiltrating our lives.

God's love for us doesn't depend on our performance or our circumstances. We don't need to try to earn His acceptance. God's love is unconditional; He accepts us just as we are. This fact isn't true only for today; it will be true for tomorrow and throughout eternity.

You may have missed a lot in your family or been betrayed by friends, but becoming secure in God's love will fill the empty spaces in your life. Are you aware of how much He loves you? Have you seen proof of His love recently?

> The Lord your God is in your midst, a victorious warrior. He will exult over you with joy, He will be quiet in His love, He will rejoice over you with shouts of joy. (Zephaniah 3:17)

God, thank You for filling the empty spaces in my life with Your unconditional love and acceptance. Nothing will ever change Your love for me. Please make me aware whenever I begin looking for love and acceptance from others, rather than receiving them from You.

Reflection Questions

Chapter 1: Seeking Love and Acceptance

1. Describe your relationship with your parents. What effect did they have on your life during your childhood and young adult years, both positive and negative? Did their investments in your life help you become a confident person? Did they convey rejection of you in a way that has affected your adult life? Explain.

2. What other family members influenced you in a positive way? How did they make you feel loved and accepted?

3. Did some family members have a negative influence on you? In what ways have they affected your view of yourself?

4. Life coach Adam Sicinski presents these symptoms of the fear of rejection:
   a. Lack of assertiveness when it comes to your social interactions
   b. Lack of courage to speak up and raise a different point of view
   c. Dissatisfaction with life, but instead of vocalizing it openly, you internalize this sadness and anger
   d. Consistently wearing different masks to please other people
   e. Feel as though other people have some kind of superiority over you
   f. Obsessed with acting and looking like other people
   g. Extremely conscious of what other people think of you
   h. Afraid to say no and express your opinion
   (For more information, see http://blog.iqmatrix.com/fear-of-rejection.)[6]

   Do you identify with some of the symptoms listed above? Place a checkmark by those symptoms. Acknowledging and accepting that you struggle with the fear of rejection will help create a willingness to take steps toward lessening that fear.

5. Do you believe an early-childhood fear of rejection has held you back from letting others know the true you? Do you seek love and acceptance by performing well? What is your response to yourself, or to others, if you don't think you were successful?

6. Review Enid's story at the end of this chapter. What was her original trigger for the fear of rejection? Describe the experience or person in your past that may be your original trigger. What emotional response did you have at that time? Think of a present experience that caused the same emotional response you had in the past.

7. To help preserve your personal discoveries as you take steps to rise above your fear of rejection, you may want to record notes and thoughts in the Journal Your Journey section (pages 160–162) or on your computer or mobile device after you finish each chapter. This will help you keep track of your experiences as you move through the three sections of this book: "Living in Captivity," "Breaking Strongholds," and "Tasting Freedom." Suggested thought questions for each section are included under question 3 of the Reflection Questions for chapter 15.

Chapter 2
Building a Wall

"Breakthrough to the next level comes only through brokenness." The keynote speaker at the 2004 Florida Christian Writers Conference grabbed my attention and didn't let go. Immediately, I somehow knew I was here for higher purposes than merely learning the craft of writing. God had brought me here to deal with my heart.

"Not your efforts, but brokenness, helps you get through to a new level," the speaker continued. "God will hit where we have built walls that keep Him at a distance. We all build walls. Sometimes God shoots a customized arrow into our hearts to wake us up."

While absorbing this declaration, I felt intense pain in my chest. With it came a sense that God had pierced my heart and said, "Your wall is keeping you at a distance from Me."

The thought that I had hurt the heart of God became unbearable. I had no idea I'd built an emotional wall of protection around my heart.

As soon as the speaker finished, I hurried from the conference room to seek aloneness in my quiet hotel room. As I knelt on the floor and buried my head in my hands, tears seeped through my fingers.

"God, I didn't know anything stood between You and me."

He revealed I had constructed a wall out of my fear of what people would think about me. That wall had become my emotional protection. My wall also blocked me from absorbing the truth that God loves me, accepts me, protects me, and delights in me. I confessed my actions as sin against God. My sorrow lifted when I opened myself to receive God's promised forgiveness.

My brokenness that night led me to the first step of unpacking the reason I feared people and how I had constructed my wall. Ideas began to flow. I reached for my briefcase and pulled out my notebook.

Soon I'd sketched a wall. I drew empty boxes at the bottom to form a foundation. In those boxes I added words that came to mind: "childhood patterns," "defense mechanisms," and "family expectations." These factors played a part in shaping who I had become.

On top of the foundation, brick by brick, I wrote the internal struggles that held me captive and determined my involuntary responses: fear of failure, fear of disappointing others, fear of not measuring up, fear of being known, need for approval, need for acceptance.

Author Paul Richardson says in his book *A Certain Risk*:

> In response to our most unforgettable heartaches, many of us have closed ourselves off, locked our hearts behind unassailable walls, and hidden away the key. Then our emotions, which God entrusted to us to be expressed purely, freely, and heartily, begin to drift, blown like a ship with a broken mast in the open sea. Eventually, some drift for so many years that we can't even imagine what it would feel like to live with reckless abandonment for God. [7]
>
> He is showing me that the greatest barriers to his artistry in and through my life are not physical dangers. . . . The real barriers are my own conjured fears and the imaginary monsters in my own closet.

These fears are phony castle walls I've constructed around me.[8]

In her book *Breaking Free*, author Beth Moore says:

> I had no idea I was in captivity until God began to set me free. If anyone had told me Christians could be in bondage, I would have argued with all the volume a person can muster when a yoke of slavery is strangling her neck. I was the worst kind of captive: a prisoner unaware. The kind of prisoner most vulnerable to her captors. The easiest prey there is. . . . A Christian is held captive by anything that hinders the abundant and effective Spirit-filled life God planned for him or her.[9]

John 10:10 says, "The thief comes only to steal and kill and destroy; I came that they may have life, and have it abundantly."

God wants us to be free to enjoy life, but I had chosen bondage. Fear of rejection caused me to hide behind my fortress. This self-imposed isolation robbed me of the joy and privilege of a life of abandonment and connecting with people. This emotional isolation applied to family members, close friends, coworkers, and even boyfriends through the years. Aloofness had become a habit, a way of life.

John Morgan, in his book *War on Fear*, said this about himself:

> I am a fairly bold guy, but that wasn't always the case. I used to blend in with the wallpaper, trying to not draw attention to myself. . . . I was a chameleon, without my own opinions or objections and without my own voice. I would say whatever I thought people wanted to hear. If life's a stage, I

hid behind my curtain of fear and only popped out when I was sure nobody would hook me around the neck and yank me off the stage. After all the taunting and abuse I suffered as a kid, my final solution was to just shut up.[10]

It's easy to unconsciously build "phony castle walls" because of our fear. We think we are protecting ourselves from people who might reject us. As a result, we are unable to relate openly to them.

Making a choice to hide from the inevitable pain and hurts of life stunts our spiritual growth. Our faith doesn't have a chance to engage in life situations, and we don't have opportunities to wrestle through our emotions as we interact with people. Our decision to live behind walls hinders God's work of transformation to mold us into the people He designed us to be.

Have you built an emotional wall of protection around yourself? What factors led to constructing a foundation for your wall? What bricks did you lay on your foundation?

> It was for freedom that Christ set us free; therefore keep standing firm and do not be subject again to a yoke of slavery. (Galatians 5:1)

Jesus, thank You for dying on the cross to set me free. I don't want to keep living in bondage and being a slave to my fear. Thank You for helping me pull down my wall.

Reflection Questions

Chapter 2: Building a Wall

Paul Richardson says: "In response to our most unforgettable heartaches, many of us have closed ourselves off, locked our hearts behind unassailable walls, and hidden away the key."

1. Do you think you have unconsciously built a wall of protection around yourself? Pray and ask God about this and record your thoughts.

2. What do you think caused you to build the wall? Describe heartaches, circumstances, experiences, or conversations that may have caused you to hide behind a wall.

3. If you realize you are hiding, sketch your wall. What factors influenced the way you built the foundation of your wall? Write those on your sketch.

4. What bricks did you lay on your unique structure's foundation? Add them to your drawing.

5. If you protect yourself from rejection by hiding behind a wall, talk with God about it. Perhaps He has some personal words to say to you, just as He did for me.

Chapter 3

Wearing a Mask

"Connie, would you pray for us as we end our class tonight?" I asked my friend who was attending the Bible study I was leading.

"It would be wonderful if you would ask someone else," she said.

Her refusal startled me. I never would have thought a woman as beautiful and poised as Connie would refuse to pray in front of others. After the closing prayer, I apologized to Connie.

"That's okay. I'm not comfortable praying out loud." She added with a laugh, "That is a mask I wear."

Intrigued, I said, "I understand about masks. Let's get together and talk about that sometime."

Dr. Pauline Rose Clance, whose research helped identify the impostor syndrome concept, says, "We sometimes create 'masks' without realizing it. We think our masks keep us safe from possible rejection. In reality, they keep us in bondage to the need to cover up who we are. Our fear keeps us from risking any revelation of our true selves. Yet, it's that revelation that may set us free."[11]

A few months after the class ended, Connie and I volunteered for the same outreach event. After carrying a batch of leftover food to the kitchen, I ran into her in the hallway.

"I'm still open to talk," I offered.

"It's . . . complicated."

"What do you mean?"

After a brief hesitation, she said, "As a child, I put on a mask as soon as I stepped out of the house. I didn't want anyone to know about my family. I felt so ashamed. I didn't even tell my best friend."

The rest of her story poured from the depths of her heart.

Every week, Connie's father traveled with his job from Tuesday to Friday, came home on Saturday and played golf, and left again the following Tuesday.

"My mother was an alcoholic," Connie confided. "Most days when I returned home from school, my mother was passed out on the sofa. Whenever I woke her up to ask to visit a friend, Mother always said no, and she often grabbed my arm, bruising me. As I grew older, I no longer asked permission."

Whenever her mother was sick with a cold or some other illness, she didn't feel like drinking. Connie enjoyed meeting her mother's needs during those days. As soon as she was well, though, her mother went back to the bottle.

Connie's two older brothers were already out of the house when Connie faced the effects of her mother's alcoholism.

During the course of Connie's growing-up days, her mother made three cruel statements to her: "I didn't intend to have you." "You were a mistake." "You are the reason I drink."

Many emotions collided inside Connie's heart as she listened to her mother's declarations of rejection. Hurt, devastation, despair, hopelessness, and a sense of abandonment rose up inside her.

At age eighteen, Connie moved into a college dorm room in another city. She had no contact with her mother, but she maintained some connection with her father during her college years and after.

One day the phone rang, and she heard her father's voice. "Connie, your mother has passed. Could you please come home?"

She dreaded going back to her childhood home, but she loved her father and desired to be a companion for him in his last years. When Connie stepped into that house and settled into her bedroom, the memories of her cruel and abusive mother descended on her like a net.

Three years later, when her father died, Connie and her two brothers gathered to discuss their dad's affairs. He had willed Connie the house and had divided the rest of the assets between the brothers.

She knew the arrangement had seemed logical to her father, so she stayed in the house, repositioned her mask, and tried her best to cope.

One bright spot appeared in her life. Peter, a friend from college who had moved back to town, wanted to date her. They began spending time together, and eventually he proposed. Connie said yes, although neither of them considered love as a reason to marry.

Peter moved into the family house after the wedding. Even though they were a couple now and were creating a new life together, Connie never viewed the house as her home. And she didn't tell him about her childhood home life.

Their two sons were born a year and a half apart. Soon after the birth of her second son, Connie realized she was in trouble emotionally and started seeing a therapist about her panic attacks. Due to the severity of her depression, the therapist recommended a week-long stay in a behavioral center. He felt this would stabilize her enough that she could return home and continue with one-on-one counseling.

However, she didn't know how to approach Peter.

He was shocked by her news. This was a difficult decision for both of them because it meant Connie had to be away from their two babies. Yet she knew it was the only way to get the help she needed. Peter cared for their sons with help from some members of their church.

During the week of her hospitalization, she received some counseling. For the first time in her life, she began to wrestle with the effects of her mother's alcoholism and abuse. She even opened up about her father's absence, which had left her feeling abandoned. Her biggest discovery: she had suffered deep emotional childhood trauma.

When she was released, though, Connie put her mask back on and returned to her role as wife and mother. She continued to receive counseling, but her purpose of seeing a therapist was to eliminate panic attacks. The counseling gave her tools to work with, and eventually the panic attacks subsided. However, their underlying cause remained.

After six years of living in the family home, she and Peter chose to build a home of their own in another city. Once they settled in and got the boys registered in school, Connie thought things would calm down inside her.

But the trauma remained.

She joined the behavioral group her therapist led. As she shared her story with the other women, reliving her childhood experiences, she began to work through the pain. Listening to the group's stories, she realized she was not alone. They'd all faced similar childhoods and suffered many of the same emotional wounds.

Today Connie feels emotionally stronger, but she doesn't think she loves Peter and her sons in a healthy, nurturing way. Her sons are not married yet. Her husband, Peter, can hardly wait for the arrival of grandchildren; Connie dreads it. She doesn't feel like a nurturing person and questions her ability to establish a good relationship with her future grandchildren.

When she finished telling me about her secret life, Connie reached out and hugged me. I believe something shifted inside her that day. She'd revealed the truth about her life, and she could tell it hadn't changed how I felt about her.

"Thank you for telling me your story, Connie," I said. "I know that reliving it was traumatic. I sense you feel you're not good enough, you don't measure up, you don't have anything to offer."

Tears welled in her eyes, affirming the truth.

"I understand why you don't feel you're a nurturing person," I said. "Your mother didn't nurture you, and you don't think you have that ability either. I felt the same inadequacy with my nephews and nieces. But God poured His love into me and equipped me to be the nurturing aunt they need. He'll do the same for you as a mother and grandmother. I see softness and a gentle spirit inside you, which are great qualities."

The effects of Connie's childhood trauma still lurk inside her. Her past has created warped stories that repeat themselves in her mind: *My life is shameful. I am not worthy or valuable enough for someone to love me. I don't know how to love others. My grandchildren won't love me.*

Do similar stories play in your mind and heart? How do they affect your view of life and your responses to others' actions and words?

God can help you rewrite those stories. He sees behind your mask; He knows who you really are. Let Him fight your fear so He can show off His masterpiece—you.

WILL THE REAL PERSON PLEASE STAND UP?

You have searched me, Lord, and you know me.
You know when I sit and when I rise; you perceive
my thoughts from afar. You discern my going out
and my lying down; you are familiar with all my
ways. Before a word is on my tongue you, Lord,
know it completely. (Psalm 139:1–4 NIV)

Lord, thank You that You understand my thoughts, my fears, and everything about me. I can't hide from You, and I don't want to. Give me courage to remove my mask, so others can understand who I am because of You.

Reflection Questions

Chapter 3: Wearing a Mask

Describe your thoughts about Dr. Clance's statement: "We sometimes create 'masks' without realizing it. We think our masks keep us safe from possible rejection. In reality, they keep us in bondage to the need to cover up who we are. Our fear keeps us from risking any revelation of our true selves. Yet, it's that revelation that may set us free."

1. How did you feel about Connie's story? Why did she hide behind a mask? What were her fears?

2. Have experiences with your family or friends caused you to defend yourself by hiding behind a mask? Describe what affect that may still have on you.

3. Do stories about fear play in your mind and heart? How do they affect your view of life and your responses to others' actions and words?

4. Do you shrink from answering questions that may reveal your true self or your past? Think about ways your choice to hide has affected your relationships.

5. Do you have one or two friends with whom you can remove your mask? What do they do or say that makes you feel secure with them?

Chapter 4
Creating a Persona

"Gail, you come across haughty."

My coworker's statement left me speechless and devastated. I didn't understand why she viewed me that way. As we talked further, she helped me realize that I had unknowingly created an aloofness and an air of superiority around me.

Though I felt confident when I joined the staff of the Campus Crusade/Cru ministry, I wanted to make sure I maintained the picture of a well-trained, efficient, organized, and capable assistant. My desire led me to create an outward persona. The downside to the facade was my tendency to hold on to it so rigidly that it blocked my emotions. I related well to my coworkers on a professional level, but did not readily open myself to them personally.

A few years later, while working and living in the Philippines, I saw the same kind of pattern emerge. At the Campus Crusade Asia headquarters, where I served as an executive assistant, I still protected myself. My well-guarded life kept me aloof and disconnected from many of my coworkers in the office. I interacted freely in our mutual work together, but kept my emotions to myself.

I maintained the same mindset while discipling young professional women in the city. I was friendly and helpful, but I didn't share personal problems or struggles. It seemed appropriate to maintain the persona of a problem-free Bible study leader.

Recently, one of my coworkers and friends from my Philippine days reminisced with me about our experiences. "You know, Gail," she said, "I don't think I ever saw you cry back then."

Her comment confirmed that I'd kept my emotions hidden all those years.

Creating a persona is a strategy that hides our real self—the self that should be able to say to a friend, "I'm struggling with something. Can we talk?"

The Cambridge Academic Content Dictionary defines *persona* as "The particular type of character that a person seems to have, which is often different from the real or private character that person has."[12]

We are perhaps aware that people see certain abilities in us, and sometimes they applaud us for our achievements. Yet, deep inside, we can't celebrate, because we are often afraid they will discover we aren't who we appear to be. This kind of fear has a name: imposter syndrome.

Dr. Christian Jarrett, a cognitive neuroscientist by training, has written books, articles, and columns in his field. In his article "Feeling like a fraud," he refers to the work of clinical psychologists Dr. Pauline Clance and Dr. Suzanne Imes, who identified the impostor syndrome in 1978. Dr. Jarrett says:

> According to Clance and Imes' seminal paper, there are three defining features of impostorism. The first is a feeling that other people have an inflated perception of your abilities. Second is a fear that your true abilities will be found out, and third is a persistent tendency to attribute successes to external factors, such as luck or disproportionate effort.[13]

Some people with impostor syndrome have a low self-esteem and therefore believe that others won't like them if they know their real abilities.

Other people excel in life, especially in their careers. Because of their skills, abilities, expertise, etc., some fill leadership roles and can become well known for their contributions to society. However, these people can lead a fear-based life and believe that, when people see what they have produced, they will be seen as frauds.

Even when they receive a compliment, they discount the accolade rather than count it as valuable, positive feedback. Their fear perpetuates a mindset that their work or contribution is not good enough. They don't consider themselves worthy of acclaim, even though they may be intelligent, capable, and creative.

Carl Richards is a financial planner, well known internationally for his sketches that have helped people understand concepts that lead to financial stability. Yet he has struggled with the effects of the imposter phenomenon.

It's at the moment when you're most vulnerable that all your doubts come crashing in around you. When I first heard that voice in my own head, I didn't know what to make of it. The fear was paralyzing. Every time I sent a sketch or something else into the world, I worried the world would say, "You're a fraud."

I was curious to learn who else suffered from it. . . . The amazing American author and poet Maya Angelou shared [that she would say to herself], "Uh oh, they're going to find out now. I've run a game on everybody, and they're going to find me out."

. . . Despite winning three Grammys and being nominated for a Pulitzer Prize and a Tony Award, this huge talent still questioned her success.

. . . I've heard that American presidents can feel this thing, too. The first time they find themselves alone in the Oval Office, they think to themselves, "I hope nobody finds out I'm in here."

. . . I think part of the impostor syndrome comes from a natural sense of humility about our work. That's healthy, but it can easily cross the line into paralyzing fear. When we have a skill or talent that has come naturally we tend to discount its value.

. . . For me, even after six years of sharing these simple sketches with the world and speaking all over the world, . . . the impostor syndrome has not gone away, but I've learned to think of it as a friend. . . . Now when I start to hear that voice in my head, I take a deep breath, pause for a minute, put a smile on my face and say, "Welcome back old friend. I'm glad you're here. Now, let's get to work." [14]

In her article "The 4 Simple Truths Imposter Syndrome Is Hiding from You," Erica Moss says,

Atlassian co-founder and co-CEO Mike Cannon-Brookes, [who] heads up a global company with thousands of employees and millions of users, [says]: "Most days, I feel like I don't really know what I'm doing."

You might look at a successful CEO and think, "How on earth can they think that when they have had so many wins?" This is because Impostor Syndrome is not based on reality, but rather a person's perception of reality.[15]

Dr. Valerie Young, founder of www.impostorsyndrome.com and national seminar speaker, says:

> There is a little voice in all of us that . . . believes we are smart, that we can do it. It's just that when we know that our work . . . will be judged, we start to second guess ourselves and our louder and more insistent impostor voice drowns out any semblance of self-assurance. "Maybe I'm really not that smart . . . maybe I really won't do that well." . . . I've worked with enough people who are truly suffering from the impostor syndrome to know they are not just "pretending" to feel like frauds.[16]

Dr. Young proclaims in her seminars that if you want to stop feeling like an imposter, you have to stop thinking like an imposter.

If we think like an imposter, we need to ask God to help us change. Instead of letting fear of rejection cause us to discount what we have accomplished, we can choose to celebrate, recognizing that God produced that work in us.

When someone offers a compliment, we no longer need to explain all the reasons we do not deserve their praise. We can simply say, "Thank you."

We have a lot to offer to others. We desire their praise; God made us worthy. Let's not try to prove ourselves worthy of our achievements or cover up who we are. We are worthy because God created us. He applauds our words and actions when done in the power of His Holy Spirit. This glorifies Him because we are proof of His life in us—our true identity.

Are you willing to let your real identity in God overrule the persona you have created?

> For I am confident of this very thing, that He who
> began a good work in you will perfect it until the
> day of Christ Jesus. (Philippians 1:6)

Father, help me surrender the persona I've created for myself and welcome the new identity You have given me as Your child. Help me focus on what You say about me, so I no longer think like an imposter.

Reflection Questions

Chapter 4: Creating a Persona

One definition of *persona* is "The particular type of character that a person seems to have, which is often different from the real or private character that person has."

1. Have you created a persona to protect yourself? Can you think of reasons you may have felt the need to do this?

2. What continues to motivate you to live behind that persona?

3. This chapter discusses the imposter syndrome related to creating a persona. Carl Richards said, "I think part of the impostor syndrome comes from a natural sense of humility about our work. That's healthy, but it can easily cross the line into paralyzing fear. When we have a skill or talent that has come naturally we tend to discount its value." Do you discount or devalue your accomplishment when someone compliments you, even when you know you deserve that compliment? Why?

4. Dr. Valerie Young says, "There is a little voice in all of us that . . . believes we are smart, that we can do it. It's just that when we know that our work . . . will be judged, we start to second guess ourselves and our louder and more insistent impostor voice drowns out any semblance of self-assurance." Have you had this kind of experience? Explain the circumstances and the results.

Chapter 5

Striving for Perfection

As soon as I opened my eyes that morning, I knew it would be a scary day.

Pulling the covers over my face, I tried to make the sun go away. A gloomy cloud mushroomed in my mind as I imagined the eyes of the students and parents focused on my clumsy legs. *I hate field day. The girls probably wish I weren't on their team.*

I finally rolled out of bed and stumbled into the kitchen. "Mom," I whined. "I wish I didn't have to go to school today."

"You'll be okay." As soon as I finished eating, she shooed me back to my bedroom.

After wiggling into my ugly blue shorts and throwing on my yellow school T-shirt, I said goodbye to Mom and reluctantly left the safety of my house. Dawdling along the three-block stretch to school, I longed to see a friend. Instead, I arrived alone.

Trudging onto the field, I spotted some fourth-grade friends who jumped up and down in their excitement. The only thing jumping in me was my heart. I slowly approached them and stood there without a word.

The time finally arrived for my teammates and me to take our places on the field for the relay race. They designated me the fourth runner, and I took my position.

The whistle blew. The first girl dashed down the field and passed the baton to the second runner. With widened eyes, I watched the second girl pass the baton to the third runner.

My heart slammed against my chest, my palms grew sweaty, and my knees felt like rubber.

The third runner sprinted toward me, extending the baton toward my open hand. As I groped for it, waves of reality battered my mind. *The other teams are ahead. I can't run fast enough. I'll be the last to finish.*

The girls yelled, "Run, Gail, run!"

Fear froze my fragile heart. *I can't do this.*

I whipped around in the opposite direction. Still holding on to the baton, I raced off the track and darted into the crowd.

My memory of that childhood day of trauma ends there. My action certainly reflects my childish attempt to avoid rejection because I didn't win the race for our team. Perhaps in my innocence I thought if people didn't see me finish last, they would forget. I must have repressed the words I most likely heard from classmates the next day.

If only I'd realized that my classmates' opinions didn't matter. I simply needed to stay in the race and run the best I could.

God isn't looking for perfection. He's not watching for our toes to cross the finish line first. His desire for us is that we experience the race.

Dr. Martin Antony and Dr. Richard Swinson, authors of *When Perfect Isn't Good Enough*, cited this definition of *perfectionists* by psychiatrist David Burns: "People . . . who strain compulsively and unremittingly toward impossible goals and who measure their own worth entirely in terms of productivity and accomplishment."[17]

Perfectionists can be found within any age bracket, family, or facet of society. If perfectionism is our strategy to cover up our insecurities and perceived inadequacies and to prove our worth, our tendency will crop up in a variety of ways.

My friend Margie relates this experience that is all too familiar for many of us:

> My four-page memoir writing assignment was due. After spending way too much time writing, editing, and rewriting, I couldn't think anymore. I read my pages to the group, and it went over well, but the instructor reminded me of my high school English teacher. She evaluated each person's memoir, pointing out the weak spots—even the mechanics—to the whole class. To me, she was stifling our freedom to express our own voices. I want to write memoirs for my family, but striving for perfection in this class about did me in.

Another friend struggled over her role as a caregiver for her mother:

> I feel I didn't do enough for my mother before she died. If I'd done things differently, it would have helped her so much more. I've had to forgive myself for being discouraged because I wasn't perfect. Romans 8:1 says, "Therefore there is now no condemnation for those who are in Christ Jesus." Since our Lord doesn't require perfection, we must not demand it of ourselves. It makes us less useable when we place some kind of convoluted trust in ourselves to do it all, rather than trusting Him to do what He wants to do through us.

Artist Julie Cameron presents some additional examples in her book *The Artist's Way*:

> The perfectionist writes, paints, creates with one eye on her audience. Instead of enjoying the process, the perfectionist is constantly grading the results.
>
> The perfectionist is never satisfied. The perfectionist never says, "This is pretty good. I think I'll just keep going."
>
> To the perfectionist, there is always room for improvement. The perfectionist calls this humility. In reality, it is egotism. It is pride that makes us want to write a perfect script.
>
> Perfectionism is not a quest for the best. *It is a pursuit of the worst in ourselves, the part that tells us that nothing we do will ever be good enough—that we should try again.*[18] (Italics mine)

Recently the perfectionist part of my personality erupted unexpectedly. Teaching a class on discovering our personal missions, I'd found the participants delightful. We had bonded as a group, and our interaction and activities brought laughter and mutual encouragement.

As I drove home, I began to evaluate the evening. This process usually helped me prepare for the next lesson. However, this night my thoughts turned inward. *You could have explained section two better. You should have helped the women interact more. They looked bored.*

Instead of trusting that God had brought about His desired results that night, I allowed my high standards of performance to discourage my heart and diminish His work. Seeking perfection centered my thoughts on myself and blocked me from seeing what the Spirit of God was doing in the lives of those women.

Dr. Saltz says:

> We are not always going to live up to our potential; we are not always going to meet our expectations or those of others. There will sometimes be humiliation, frustration, and anger. . . . If we are really, really terrified of feeling like a failure, we'll pull back and not invest ourselves. We'll settle for that job that is less than we could achieve because it is a way of avoiding pain at all costs. But we will also have to forfeit the joy and confidence that come with having worked hard at something and having succeeded. We will have to live with that sinking sense of not ever having tested ourselves to see how much we could accomplish in our lives.[19]

Perfectionism finds its roots in the belief that others will accept us only if we perform perfectly. That mindset prevents us from accepting what we view as a less-than-perfect completion of our goals. Unfortunately, giving in to that kind of thinking perpetuates a trust in ourselves rather than God.

What happens if our boss, coworker, spouse, family member, or friend—anyone to whom we look for approval—makes us feel we haven't performed well? That encounter can trigger the same emotions we may have felt as a child, either within our family or through a personal experience, because we think we didn't meet their expectation.

When perfection is our goal, we can become fanatical about doing well so we will receive the positive feedback we crave. When we see no indication of approval, we usually feel like a failure. As a result, we can't celebrate what we did contribute.

Someone suggested we ask ourselves this honest question: Suppose the person from whom we seek approval or praise gave us what we think we need. Would that remedy the broken part inside us that led us to perform for them?

My honest answer is no. I'd still be tempted to perform.

What would your answer be? When you unravel the reasons for your performance-oriented life, what do you find?

> O Lord, You are my God; I will exalt You, I will give thanks to Your name; for You have worked wonders, plans formed long ago, with perfect faithfulness. (Isaiah 25:1)

Lord, help me give up trying to be perfect. I want to do my best and trust in Your plans, which are perfect for me.

Reflection Questions

Chapter 5: Striving for Perfection

1. We learned this definition of *perfectionists*: "People . . . who strain compulsively and unremittingly toward impossible goals and who measure their own worth entirely in terms of productivity and accomplishment." Do you fit that definition? If so, in what areas of your life is perfectionism most obvious?

2. When you unravel the reasons for your performance-oriented life, what do you find?

3. Can you think of an example when you pulled back from a risk, an opportunity, or an assignment because you were afraid you might not do it perfectly?

4. Have you moved forward or jumped into a situation even though you weren't sure of the result? What effect did that choice have on your thinking and actions afterward?

5. What was your response to this question at the end of this chapter? "Suppose the person from whom we seek approval or praise gave us what we think we need. Would that remedy the broken part inside us that led us to perform for them?" Based on your answer, do you want to make changes in your life?

6. Now that you have finished the chapters in "Living in Captivity" and have considered your answers to the Reflection Questions, do you have additional discoveries and experiences you want to record in the Journal Your Journey section (pages 160–162) or on your computer or mobile device? You may want to look at the suggestions included in question 3 of the Reflection Questions for chapter 15.

Part Two
Breaking Strongholds

Chapter 6
Releasing Perceptions

"I'm dreading this weekend, Lord."

Janice always looked forward to her morning times with God in her Florida sunroom. Today, though, thoughts about the upcoming weekend with her husband's extended family disturbed her peace.

She had never felt loved or accepted by Bob's family. Every time she saw them, she sensed nothing but rejection. Their words, actions, and facial expressions convinced her she didn't measure up.

Bob knew her feelings. This time Janice had no choice but to travel with him to Princeton for the celebration of her stepdaughter's hooding and commencement for her PhD.

Janice poured out her heart to God that morning, and He answered.

Why?

"I'm afraid."

What are you afraid of?

"I'm afraid I'll be hurt, and I'm afraid I'll fight back and say something I'll regret."

Immediately, Isaiah 41:10 flooded her mind: *Do not fear, for I am with you; do not anxiously look about you, for I am your God. I will strengthen you, surely I will help you, surely I will uphold you with My righteous right hand.*

After reading that passage, she realized God was going to Princeton with her. He would strengthen her in the power of the Holy Spirit. Her burden lifted, and she was no longer afraid.

After the event, Janice shared these results with me:

> The weekend wasn't comfortable, but it was okay because I no longer feared what I would say or do if my in-laws were unkind. I saw a change in me from the beginning. I took the initiative to greet someone who had been unkind to me in the past.
>
> Another person had always hurt me, no matter what he said. I'd always taken offense at his words. This time I didn't.
>
> I was amazed at my peace of mind and lack of defensiveness. Even though God tells me I shouldn't fight back with my words, I don't always obey. Fighting back had become my defense mechanism. That weekend God gave me the ability to reach out to those I normally would not have spoken to. Even when people were less than cordial, I chose not to take their attitude personally.

John Morgan says,

> A stronghold is a deeply embedded thought pattern that attempts to keep you from the path God has for you. . . . It's a furrow or a groove in your brain that sends thoughts habitually down a harmful path.
>
> The good news is that along with these low roads and strongholds there is the high road. Spiritually, rather than our thoughts being led down a

stronghold's groove, we can fill in the stronghold ditch with the truth of God. . . .

That's why the psalmist said, "I have hidden your word in my heart. . . ." (Ps.119:11 NIV) and Jesus said, "You will know the truth, and the truth will set you free" (John 8:32 NIV). Rather than being a prisoner to fear or the emotions it causes, we can be free.[20]

Like many of us, Janice's thoughts kept her imprisoned. As she struggled with her husband's family's feelings about her, the thoughts *They don't like me, I will never be accepted,* and *Nothing I say will be right* consumed her. Every time they got together, fear crept in and hindered her from being herself around them.

The apostle Paul reminds us to use God's weapons in our fight against our thoughts:

> For though we walk in the flesh, we do not war according to the flesh, for the weapons of our warfare are not of the flesh, but divinely powerful for the destruction of fortresses. We are destroying speculations and every lofty thing raised up against the knowledge of God, and we are taking every thought captive to the obedience of Christ. (2 Corinthians 10:3–5)

Janice used God's Word as her "weapon." Because she believed God's promise that He would go with her, she released her fear to Him. Once her perspective changed, she experienced confidence to be kind, no matter what words she heard or attitudes she observed. Her new way of thinking continued to make a difference in her relationships with her husband's family.

Beth Moore is committed to helping believers tear down strongholds. These strongholds keep us imprisoned by our thoughts and cause us to focus on people's opinions of us rather than on the truth of how God sees us.

Beth says:

> Virtually anything that cheats you of what God has for you could be considered sin. Once we are willing to see the sin involved in the stronghold and agree with God through confession, we begin to see the lies surrounding us. Tearing down the lies wallpapering our minds causes the prison door to swing open.
>
> Satan does not have the power or authority to lock believers in a prison of oppression, but he works overtime to talk us into staying. . . .
>
> Picture the captivity of our thought life like a prison cell wallpapered in lies. Demolition of strongholds really begins when we expose and tear down the lies fueling our stronghold. . . .
>
> Taking thoughts captive to Christ doesn't mean we never have the thought again. It means we learn to "think the thought" as it relates to Christ and who we are in Him.[21]

Remember Enid's story in chapter 1? She received three dramatic rejections during her school years. Those experiences, which ruled her thoughts and fueled her fear of desertion by her friends, kept her in bondage. Enid tells us how God began to set her free:

During the kindergarten experience, Andrew rescued me from having to play alone after my two friends intentionally left me out of their games.

Andrew was my rescuer that day, but later, Jesus became my permanent Rescuer. It happened at a special student event on my college campus. That night, some friends and I strolled to the gathering, glad for a reason to get out of our dorm rooms.

A woman welcomed us and talked about God, using pictures of nature. At the end of her presentation, she asked people to come forward if they wanted to pray. I stayed in my seat.

Afterward, I approached the woman and told her I definitely wanted to know God. But I didn't see how I could because I had done things that displeased God. She showed me 1 John 1:9 ("If we confess our sins, He is faithful and righteous to forgive us our sins and to cleanse us from all unrighteousness"). Then she helped me pray for forgiveness and accept Jesus as my Savior and Lord.

This wonderful experience happened shortly before my college boyfriend rejected me. My Christian friends wondered how I would respond as a new Christian.

I took my broken heart to Jesus. He reminded me of God's love and promise in Hebrews 13:5: "I will never desert you, nor will I ever forsake you." My boyfriend deserted me, but I knew my Rescuer never would. That truth helped heal my heart. My friends were amazed.

Whenever I struggle with the fear of people rejecting me, Jesus overpowers my fear by reminding me that He will rescue me in every situation. The stories I told myself all those years—that I wasn't lovable and, therefore, people would leave me—are being rewritten.

We are complex people with a variety of early experiences that influence us today. Our genetic makeup determines, to some extent, how we will respond to life situations. However, our subconscious stores all our experiences and weaves stories to explain what happened to us. But our subconscious cannot tell the difference between what occurred fifteen minutes ago and what occurred fifteen years ago.

These inner stories, over which we have no control, program us to respond in certain ways, especially if we have been disappointed or wounded or rejected. They play over and over in our minds, telling us who we are or are not, how we should react to people, and which people are safe for us.

Even though these stories exist below the surface of our consciousness, they permeate our personalities and our lives, keeping our fears and perceived incompetence alive.

The stories evolve in our subconscious when an emotional need is not filled or when we're blocked from expressing our true selves. Always at the center of them is a denial of the four basic human core needs:

- The need to attach
- The need to become individuals
- The need to express ourselves
- The need to be accepted for who we are

As we consider how to release our perceptions, we naturally think about our experiences within our families. We want our parents and other family members to love and accept us. When we believe they don't, our perception of that reality keeps us in captivity. We feel it's too risky to come out of hiding and be honest about how we feel. As a result, our four basic core needs are left unfulfilled.

As you know, I didn't feel close to Aunt Elia. Some of my doubts about her love for me centered on her criticism. A lot of her corrections related to proper use of grammar in my speech and writing. Our entire family valued the use of good grammar and felt free to correct one another. In my opinion, Aunt Elia took her role to an extreme with me.

When I lived in the Philippines, I mailed her a copy of my bimonthly newsletter since she and my uncle were part of my ministry team. After reading each one, she used a red pen to correct my grammar. Then she mailed the newsletter back to me, even though it required a high-priced overseas stamp. This pattern continued for years.

One day, after opening and reading yet another corrected letter, I worked up my nerve to send her a note. I explained how difficult it was to receive her corrections, in hopes that she would stop.

My mother wrote that Aunt Elia was hurt by my letter. I immediately felt guilty. Rather than standing my ground in expressing the truth of how I felt, I bought her a gift from the Filipino market and included a note, apologizing for hurting her. I continued to receive corrections.

Many years later, when I moved back to the US, she continued to critique my newsletters. Soon it expanded to emails. One time, I noticed a word she used incorrectly. I pointed it out. Immediately, she emailed back to explain the reason she had chosen that word.

It seemed like a losing battle. God surprised me by softening my heart toward her and prompting me to send a different kind of email: "Aunt Elia, we can continue to correct each other's emails and letters, but isn't our relationship more important than that?" I don't remember receiving a response, but her corrections stopped, and our relationship began to shift.

God gave me courage to let go of my long-ingrained perception of Aunt Elia and speak to her more honestly. I chose to believe she loved me and her corrections were her way of trying to help me.

This change of heart and my honest email to her helped fulfill my four core needs:

- The need to attach: I created an opportunity for us to attach as niece and aunt, not as a writer being reprimanded by her editor.
- The need to become an individual: I interacted with confidence and assumed the right to be my own person rather than relate to her as a child.
- The need to express myself: instead of burying my feelings of shame about disappointing her and trying to do better in the future, I wrote to her with honesty. She knew I no longer wanted to play that game.
- The need to be accepted for who I am: I gave her a chance to accept me, even if I made mistakes.

By releasing the perception that Aunt Elia's corrections meant she didn't love me, I was able to establish a closer relationship with her. I felt more comfortable and less guarded, which made it easier to express love to her.

Something shifted in her as well. One specific change I noticed was one sentence she began to write in cards and letters: "I'm proud of you." Those precious words of affirmation filled my heart. Our mutual love set a new tone in our relationship for the rest of her life.

Our perceptions of people and situations affect our responses. We cannot prevent our subconscious from weaving stories about how we should think and respond to life. However, when negative or fearful thoughts rise to the surface because of those inner stories, we can surrender them to God. He will destroy those thoughts because they go against His will for us.

Do stories still replay in your mind and hinder you from freedom to enjoy close relationships? Or are you making progress in rewriting those stories by believing what God's Word says about you? This truth sets us free to be more honest and open with people about ourselves. Becoming a more genuine person leads to healthier relationships centered on love and acceptance.

> Jesus was saying to those Jews who had believed Him, "If you continue in My word, then you are truly disciples of Mine; and you will know the truth, and the truth will make you free."
> (John 8:31–32)

God, thank You for Your Word, which reveals truth and sets me free from false beliefs. Help me release my perceptions to You so I can freely enjoy my relationships with other people without being concerned about what they think.

Reflection Questions

Chapter 6: Releasing Perceptions

1. Are you holding on to certain perceptions about a family member, a coworker, a neighbor, or another friend? Describe your thoughts.

2. Do you listen to stories replaying in your mind, telling you what people think of you? What do some of those stories say? Do they prevent you from enjoying close and healthy relationships with those people?

3. Are you making progress in rewriting your stories and becoming more honest and open about who you are and what you think? Describe some changes you have seen.

4. In the opening story about Janice, how did her perceptions affect her behavior around her husband's family? What enabled her to let go of those thoughts?

5. Reread 2 Corinthians 10:3–5. How can God's Word help you recognize your human thoughts and release them to God?

6. Have you begun to focus more on the truth of God's thoughts toward you rather than other people's? Find some verses that show you how God views you. Use these reminders in a special prayer time with God.

7. As you begin this new section, "Breaking Strongholds," stay aware of your transformation as God helps you break each stronghold that kept you in bondage. You will want to record your personal experiences in the Journal Your Journey section (pages 160–162) or on your computer or mobile device.

Chapter 7
Letting the Bricks Fall

The visit of Piper, my nine-year-old curly-haired niece, was coming to an end.

That afternoon, she and her dad, Casey, drove across town to do one last activity together before heading home. After they left, I sat down at the dining table to do some work.

While waiting for my computer to boot up, I observed her playthings scattered across my living room. Colorful sticky notes filled up with her hand-drawn pictures and profound sayings covered half of the dining table.

Suddenly, tears rained on my cheeks, unfamiliar emotions bubbling up in me. I had never loved anyone the way I loved Piper in that moment. I whispered, "I'll miss you, Piper. I'll really miss you."

She had played with me and teased me, ignorant of my fears and feelings of inadequacy to relate well as her aunt. Her facial expressions, laughter, and creativity pulled me into her world of carefree oblivion of others' opinions. With her, I didn't have to act a certain way or say the right things. She accepted me simply as Aunt Gail.

Piper's love had cut through many of my emotional issues. She had created a new space in my heart and poured unconditional love into it. God didn't want me to hide those new emotions of love. Rather, He prompted me to express them to her.

When Piper and Casey returned from their excursion, I listened to her excitement. Then I took her hand. "I want to tell you something. Let's go sit together on the couch."

When we'd made ourselves comfortable, I looked into her blue eyes and gazed at her sweet face. "I want you to know how much I love you. I'll really miss you when you leave. I'm going to keep all of your notes to remind me of you."

Piper listened, keeping her focus on me. She smiled, but didn't respond with words or hugs. But she usually didn't, so I wasn't surprised.

She always let me hug her when she arrived and when she left, but never responded with much enthusiasm. I pondered the reason for that, especially since she and her dad were affectionate with each other. Maybe she didn't receive many hugs from her mother during the times she stayed with her.

After packing the car together, I hugged Casey goodbye and walked around to Piper's open door. I smiled at her and leaned forward for a hug. This time she wrapped her small arms around my neck and hugged me tightly.

Thank You, God. She understood.

"Aunt Gail, are you going to your bedroom when we leave?"

"Probably."

"Well, look on your bed. There's a surprise for you."

After waving goodbye, I made my way to my bedroom. On the bedspread sat a small yellow sticky note that said, "Go to your computer & see the surprise there. Piper ☺"

Hurrying to my computer, I spotted three more yellow notes spaced out below the keyboard.

"I love you ~ Piper."

"I will miss you, Aunt Gail ~ Love, Piper."

"Sorry we could not stay longer ~ Love, Piper."

I cried again. Each of her written notes matched what I had expressed to her verbally. Through that intimate exchange in our own personal love languages, we connected on a deeper level.

After enjoying their visits and building new memories together, I usually waved goodbye, went back inside to put away the playthings, and returned to my normal life.

Not this time. It was months before I could bear to put away the cardboard ticket booth Piper and I had created. It sat on the floor next to my piano, where she'd performed her concert. Her colorful notes still covered half of my dining table.

This little girl changed my heart, helping to break down the remaining bricks in my wall. I'd never before been able to love my family and friends deeply, engage with them emotionally, and blend my life with theirs.

Piper gave me courage to love her and other family members freely and unconditionally. I cherish this new feeling of awe and wonder and desire. I pray daily that my newly expressed love will remain in Piper's heart. Her sweet love certainly found a permanent place in mine.

In chapter 2, I told you about my experience at the writers' conference when God pierced my heart with His customized arrow. That night, God showed me I was imprisoned by my wall. My guarded emotions caused an aloofness with people and with Him. In my brokenness, I asked God to set me free.

The tearing down of my wall has been a gradual and unique process made possible by the courage and strength God pours into me. After my escape from the concrete walls of self-protection, I wrote a poem to capture the difference it made.

Real Life

An arrow pierced my heart.
Through the blackened hole,
My buried self climbed out,
Breaking my armor of aloofness,
Knocking over towers of timidity.

Once outside castle windows
And defensive walls,
I gasped for breath,
Afraid of death,
In the valley of vulnerability.

Slowly fear gave way to hope
As I viewed God's landscape.
Colorful blossoms beckoned to me,
Crowding out the memory
Of concrete security.

Reality dawned:
Wide-open spaces,
Freedom to move,
No reason to hide.

Taking one step forward,
I began my new journey
Toward real life.

gp 1997

Ephesians 2:13–14 says, "But now in Christ Jesus you who formerly were far off have been brought near by the blood of Christ. For He Himself is our peace, who made both groups into one and broke down the barrier of the dividing wall."

We've tried our own method of protection by building a wall, but it produced only isolation, continued fear, and lack of relationship. With God's strength, we can leave our useless castle behind. Even when we first step out into that valley of vulnerability, God will shield us with His armor.

> Finally, be strong in the Lord and in the strength of His might. Put on the full armor of God, so that you will be able to stand firm against the schemes of the devil. For our struggle is not against flesh and blood, but against the rulers, against the powers, against the world forces of this darkness, against the spiritual forces of wickedness in the heavenly places. Therefore, take up the full armor of God, so that you will be able to resist in the evil day, and having done everything, to stand firm.
> (Ephesians 6:10–13)

My constant prayer is that God will make me aware of the ways He is working in my life as I enjoy my new landscape.

One answer to this prayer came through spending time with Shirley, a close friend for more than forty years. We met during our first jobs in California and continued our friendship during our mutual careers in the Philippines. We began staying in touch by email after we both returned to the US, but we hadn't seen each other for years.

Since I was going to be in Portland for a short visit and Shirley lived on the Oregon coast, we decided to meet halfway for an overnight. Even though this meant a three-hour drive for both of us, we were determined not to miss the chance for a face-to-face visit.

At the end of our uplifting visit, we both were at a loss when it came time to say goodbye.

"Gail, you've changed," Shirley said. "You're not the prim and proper woman I've always known."

"Really, Shirley? Am I that different?"

"The difference in the way you got out of your car yesterday was amazing. Before, you would have primly and properly swung your feet out and risen as a lady should. However, when you saw me waiting, you jumped out of your car, came running up to me, and threw your arms around me in a tight hug."

"I didn't even think about what I was doing because I was excited to see you," I said. "I'm glad if I seemed less inhibited."

"You walk, talk, and express yourself so differently. Immediately, I knew something had changed. You were so free and joyful! Your usual hesitation and guardedness are gone."

I remember clasping my hands together in childlike delight, amazed at her descriptions. With tears and a smile, I hugged Shirley. "Thank you for telling me. Your words confirm that I am truly out of prison, and God is changing my life. I'm excited."

The new emotions and freedom Shirley saw in me surprised her. They still surprise me.

The following dialogue from a fiction book describes other changes that have transpired in my life:

> I'm hoping, praying, that the wall you've had to put in place around yourself and your emotions will come down. That there will be more of *you* appearing. Wider emotional swings both up and

down. More energy. Dreams for your life. Things you want. Desires of the heart. . . . The more of [life] you are *feeling*, the closer you are to being whole again.

. . . It will give you the ability to see the world around you as it exists both good and bad. It will be having a life that isn't being steered by the past, where it doesn't feel like the past is a daily anchor weighing on your thoughts, or on your impressions of places and people. Healing will bring the capacity and the ability to love family and care about friends. It will be about having dreams for yourself and the confidence to work toward them. Healing in part is being able to *feel* you are free of the past.[22]

When we let the bricks fall from our walls, more emotions will rise to the surface. This will feel unfamiliar to us at first. Embrace those emotions because they are part of our healing.

Our new vulnerability in open spaces may seem scary, but each new step forward takes us further from captivity and closer to the freedom God desires us to experience. We have been in isolation too long.

Piper helped me tear down the rest of my wall and come out of my isolation from people. When she drew me into her life, deep emotions came out of me that I hadn't experienced before. My new love for her gave me courage to open myself to others as well.

I believe God touched her heart also. Because I could express my love and connect with her on a deeper level, Piper felt she had permission to love me in a new way too. Maybe she had been holding back from hugging me and other family members because she didn't know how we would respond. I hope our heartfelt hugs will continue to be a high point in our relationship as aunt and niece.

Have you let the bricks crumble from your wall? God has new people for you to meet and new adventures for you to experience.

> You are my hiding place; you will protect me from trouble and surround me with songs of deliverance. (Psalm 32:7 NIV)

Father, I ask You to deliver me from my prison. Please lead me to Your hiding place where You will protect me and also equip me to help set other people free.

Reflection Questions

Chapter 7: Letting the Bricks Fall

1. When we put up a wall that keeps us at a distance from others, it naturally affects our relationships. We are guarded— as I was with my niece, Piper—and we keep our emotions inside. Can you think of a person whom you love but have not felt secure enough to reveal to them your thoughts and emotions? Name that person. Pray and ask God to give you courage to express what is inside you so you can build a closer and more authentic relationship.

2. God is the One who will tear down the wall for you. Are you willing for Him to do that? Do you believe He will protect you emotionally, mentally, physically, and spiritually?

3. Reread Ephesians 6:10–13. Do the truths in this passage change your perspective about the kind of battle you face now? Describe the changes in your thinking.

4. Also read Ephesians 6:14–17. What are the six parts of God's armor? To fight the spiritual battles that keep us in bondage, we need to put on all His armor daily by repeating each part of the armor aloud as we pray to Him. If necessary, for a while, make a daily note on your calendar to include this in your prayer time with God.

Chapter 8
Taking Off the Mask

Surrender always involves risk. One night, at a Cru US Staff Conference, I discovered how much.

As the lights dimmed, emcee Kim Anthony[23] walked to the center of the stage. The huge crowd waited. As if talking to only one person, she opened her heart and revealed the following personal journey:

> I've enjoyed coming to staff conferences for seventeen years in relative obscurity. As an introvert, I was always excited and happy to lay low, sit at the feet of Jesus, and sip my mint tea.
>
> About a year ago, I began to sense God asking me if I were willing to give up my anonymity for Him. It took me a long time to respond. When I did, I said yes to His invitation to join Him in what He is doing in our ministry. I knew that even in my own insecurities, He would be with me.
>
> A few days later, after I fully surrendered, I received a call from the conference team asking me to consider this role. It took me even longer to get back to them.
>
> I hesitated because a little girl in me, who grew up in the Hood surrounded by drugs, tried to convince me I didn't belong. A teenage girl in me tried to stand up and beg me to run away.

Still, after much prayer, I said yes.

Those wounded places may still rise up during this week, but I have determined ahead of time to stand up no matter how uncomfortable it may be.

When Kim finished her story, silence reigned among five thousand staff members crowded into endless rows of green plastic seats in Colorado State's Moby Gym. We heard no rustling, no coughing. Everyone seemed to be taking in the raw honesty they had just witnessed.

I, too, sat immobilized, oblivious to the people next to me. I couldn't wrap my mind around what I'd just seen and heard: Kim, an introvert, standing courageously in front of that enormous crowd and revealing her deep feelings.

Suddenly, God presented me with the same question He had asked Kim. *Are you willing to give up your anonymity—take off your mask—for Me?*

I flinched at the thought. An introvert myself, I remembered the times God pushed me out of my comfort zone. Each adventure into the unknown created initial trauma. Yet afterward, I knew God had created that opportunity to expand my horizons.

Most recently, God had asked me to let go of my ministry with Cru/Campus Crusade and step into a new journey. I prayed about and pondered this unexpected challenge because it would take me away from the only ministry I'd known for fifty years. In the end, I knew this was a good plan from God, a journey He had ordained to enlarge my ministry. With peace in my heart, I said yes.

The realization hadn't sunk in, though, that having my own personal ministry in Orlando might expose me to greater visibility. There in the darkness, I couldn't ignore this reality.

Tears escaped from my eyes as thoughts collided. *I'm not comfortable with being known and standing in the limelight. What if people discover that I don't deserve to be there?*

None of it mattered to God in that sacred moment in His presence. He flooded me with love and peace and the courage to whisper, "Yes, I'm willing." Even though my surrender would involve new risks, I placed my trust in the God who knows my name and my fears.

God wants me to throw off my facade, stand up, and speak for Him as Kim had. In those moments, He reminded me of His promise to give me words to say and confidence to be who I am.

Then He whispered something in my heart I'll never forget: *You don't have to be perfect. You don't have to be right. You just have to be Mine.*

A few months after I returned to Orlando, a formal invitation to a gala celebration appeared in my email box. The invitation wasn't a surprise, but the details of my personal involvement shook me. I would need to stand on stage at the Garden Theatre in my "most glamorous gown" to be introduced to the audience who would gather to help launch Judy Johnson's book *Fascinating Women: Living by Faith.*

Judy had selected my story, along with thirty others, to include in her new book. When she first presented her plan, I said, "Judy, I'm not a fascinating woman."

"In my eyes, you are. I love your adventure of serving God overseas for more than twenty years as a single woman. I want others to see your faith, so let me interview you and write your story."

With the book now published, Judy confirmed her upcoming celebration. She described the event as only she could: "Vintage movie theater, beautiful ambience, charming venue that speaks glamour and excitement. 'Fascinating Women' will appear on the marquee."

An introvert friend and I—both deemed "fascinating women" because of our stories in Judy's book—commiserated together prior to the gala. "This gala affair isn't us. It's way out of our comfort zone." Later, our anticipation grew when we realized God wanted us to participate to honor Judy.

The time of the celebration arrived. After a short time of getting acquainted in a side room, we "fascinating women" circulated among more than a hundred guests in the aisles of the auditorium.

On stage, an old-fashioned wing chair had been placed beside a small table boasting a colorful bouquet of flowers. This would become Judy's vantage spot while she orchestrated the multiple portions of the program.

Excitement mounted. The first important moment arrived. Judy's announcement floated above the chattering: "The twelve fascinating women are going to gather up front now to sign their chapter in the book."

Quickly a line formed down one aisle, leading to the first fascinating woman. After securing the desired autograph, each guest moved to the next fascinating woman. Natural conversation floated around the room, delight obvious in the faces. This was a book signing like no other.

When Judy called time, we slowly wound our way back to our seats. The room quieted, and Judy called us forward in groups of four.

When my time came, I stood and approached the front. Taking the hand of one of Judy's handsome grandsons, I climbed the stairs and walked across the stage to hug her.

What a privilege to stand next to this beautiful, loving, and courageous woman. She had remained faithful to God throughout her life, even in the midst of a recent diagnosis of pancreatic cancer that would claim her life four months later.

After listening to Judy tell the audience about our special friendship as writers, I received the mic and turned with confidence toward the audience. Smiling with the joy God placed inside me, I presented my update with words that highlighted His faithfulness in my life.

When the presentations were complete, the twelve of us followed the photographer's instructions. Our group picture marked a historic occasion for Judy and everyone in that room. The whole affair will surely be talked about for years to come.

That day I would rather have remained anonymous and blended in with the audience. However, God had been showing me how to live in freedom rather than fear. This beautiful event gave me one of my first opportunities to give up my anonymity since surrendering it to Him.

My friend Sharon, a public-school teacher, had lived an anonymous life for years. As an introvert, this was her choice. Then God began creating ways to pull her out of her comfort zone. Here is her story:

> Extreme shyness is one weakness I couldn't avoid during my growing-up years. I hid behind my mask of shyness for fear of being wrong, rejected, or ridiculed. I didn't even talk at school, except to neighborhood friends.
>
> As a college student, I became involved with the Campus Crusade staff team. Gradually, I learned to take risks such as leading discipleship studies and sharing Christ with my friends. When the

leader asked me to join the student speaker team, I couldn't believe I agreed. What gave me courage was knowing I could depend on the Holy Spirit to overcome my fear.

After five years of ministering to college students as a full-time staff member of Campus Crusade, I became a public-school teacher. Surprisingly, in that school setting, I reverted to my emotional experiences from elementary and high school days.

My shyness returned in full bloom. I built friendships with other teachers but never said a word in staff meetings.

Years later, Linda, the school principal, discovered a research paper I had written. She asked, "Sharon, would you please share your discoveries with the staff?"

God gave me courage to accept her invitation. Linda was happy about my presentation and the eagerness of the teachers to implement my ideas for increasing literacy.

Eventually, Linda posed another question to me: "Have you ever thought of being an elementary-school principal?"

That brought to mind an experience I'd had several years before while working late in my classroom. I heard a voice in my head: *You are going to be a principal someday.* That didn't make sense, because I still battled shyness and maintained a low profile in my job.

God used Linda's question to confirm that He had a new direction for me. Two years later, after completing my master's degree and receiving the necessary license, I was asked to interview for a principal position in a nearby city.

The interview included a fifty-minute oral presentation to a panel of seventeen people, followed by a sixty-minute question-and-answer session. Once I began talking, I relaxed and spoke with new self-assurance.

After seeing all the evaluations, Linda called me. "Sharon, I'm so excited. You're the only applicant who received the top score of ten on every question."

I was hired.

Talking at staff meetings and parent-teacher meetings, as well as school assemblies, graduations, etc., became part of my life. My confidence in public speaking comes from my dependence on God's power to overcome my weakness.

I no longer need to hide behind my mask of shyness. God has introduced me to a new way of life.

We wear masks to cover up our feelings of insecurity and self-doubt, which are fed by our inner stories. That way, we can hide our weaknesses and shameful pasts. God wants us to take off our masks, come out of hiding, and allow people to know the person He created us to be. Once we are willing to reveal the new person we are today, we become proof that God can overcome and overpower anything that happened to us in the past.

You may remember Connie from chapter 3, where she told her story about her abusive and alcoholic mother and her traveling dad who left her feeling abandoned. All her life, Connie wore a mask to keep people from knowing about her family. She didn't tell even her best friend, and she withheld her story from her husband until many years into their marriage.

Recently, when she removed her mask long enough to share her past, she tasted her first moments of freedom. Her secret was out.

Dr. Richardson says,

> Our relationships with one another . . . erupt with life when we find one another's souls. Some call this way of life "being transparent." Others refer to it as showing one's true colors. I call it veracity—a way of life that is continually stripping off the enslaving masks that weigh down our souls and journeying with God in the freedom of truth, even if that truth sometimes hurts.[24]

Connie and I plan to get together and review what she learned as a participant in the women's group. Perhaps when she recalls that God uniquely designed her and created her for a special purpose, she will have the courage to believe the truth: she is a worthy and valuable person because God is her life. I hope she will no longer believe the lie that her home life defines her.

I'm praying that Connie will allow others the opportunity to know this wonderful person who has been living behind a mask. She told me she senses God is going to use her painful and traumatic life as a platform for bringing His hope to other women in similar situations.

King David said to God:

> You make known to me the path of life; you will fill me with joy in your presence, with eternal pleasures at your right hand. (Psalm 16:11 NIV)

God has a wonderful and uniquely designed path for each of us to follow. When we trust God, take off our masks, and give up our anonymity, our choice leads to a path of freedom. We no longer need to try to be what other people want us to be. We are free to stand up and be recognized for who we are.

Father, show me the path You want me to follow. Today I take off my mask and surrender my fear to You. Because of You, I can stand up with confidence and let others know who You made me to be.

Reflection Questions

Chapter 8: Taking Off the Mask

1. Do you wear a mask to keep people from seeing the real you or knowing your past?

2. Are you comfortable being seen? Or do your circumstances or personality make it difficult for you to step forward and be visible?

3. Have you ever had to decide whether to accept a frightening opportunity that would put you in the limelight? Describe the details. What made you afraid or hesitant? What was the outcome?

4. What if God asked you, "Are you willing to give up your anonymity—take off your mask—for Me?" How would you respond to Him? Your answer may affect your life in different ways. It could relate to a one-time commitment in which you will be noticed. Or it might involve continual visibility through a new role.

5. Brainstorm the opportunities in front of you. What factors hold you back from saying yes? How will saying yes help you fight your fear of rejection?

6. Dr. Richardson describes being truthful as "a way of life that is continually stripping off the enslaving masks that weigh down our souls and journeying with God in the freedom of truth, even if that truth sometimes hurts." Describe the small steps you could take to become more transparent and honest, so you can build authentic relationships.

Chapter 9
Leaving the Persona Behind

I wondered what new experiences waited for me on this special return to Asia. More than ten years had passed since I'd lived and worked on that continent.

My original purpose for being there had been clearly defined. However, God had something more in store for me.

Cru's East Asia Orient teams had gathered at the Taiwan hotel for their annual planning conference. At the beginning of the first session, the screen flashed the names of people who would have a part in the program. When I saw my name, I thought, *Why am I on that list? I'm not an up-front speaker. I'm ministering to the women for only one evening.*

They asked all of us to come to the front so they could introduce us and pray for us. I had to go forward and explain what I would be doing, but I didn't feel qualified to stand there.

I had been invited to preview *The Significant Woman*[25] course during one of the dinners. Since I had co-authored this life-coaching discipleship course, I always enjoyed the chance to help women in various countries experience a portion of the content. These previews are designed to help equip women to facilitate their own small groups. To me, this was a welcome, behind-the-scenes opportunity.

Following a day of workshops, we reassembled in the meeting room for the evening session. The speaker centered his message on God's commendation and admonition to the seven churches in Asia listed in the book of Revelation.

While talking about the church in Pergamum, Dr. Lawrence said, "The thing God had against this church was that they practiced idolatry."

With pain in my heart, I realized I was practicing idolatry. I was a people pleaser.

I sat ramrod-straight in my chair, staring into space, my arms loose at my sides. The truth of my sin engulfed me. Silently I confessed my sin to God, agreeing that I cared more about pleasing people than pleasing Him.

Sorrow for grieving God gave way to a longing to be free from my idolatry. Soon, the peace of forgiveness filled my heart. God assured me He had heard my prayer and would help set me free.

Edward T. Welch, author of *When People Are Big and God Is Small*, explains:

> What is it that shame-fear and rejection-fear have in common? . . . They both indicate that people are our favorite idol. . . . We worship them as ones who have God-like ability to "fill" us with esteem, love, admiration, acceptance. . . .
>
> What we fear shows our allegiances. It shows where we put our trust. It shows who is big in our lives.[26]

I became aware of the speaker's voice again. "You will remember the miraculous feeding of the four thousand. Later, Jesus and His disciples got in the boat and began rowing to the other side."

He read Mark 8:14–21 to us:

> And [the disciples] had forgotten to take bread, and did not have more than one loaf in the boat with them. . . . And they began to discuss with one another the fact that they had no bread. And Jesus, aware of this, said to them, "Why do you discuss the fact that you have no bread? Do you not yet see or understand? Do you have a hardened heart? . . . And do you not remember, when I broke the five loaves for the five thousand, how many baskets full of broken pieces you picked up?" They said to Him, "Twelve." "And when I broke the seven for the four thousand, how many large baskets full of broken pieces did you pick up?" And they said to Him, "Seven." And He was saying to them, "Do you not yet understand?"

Bill lifted his eyes from his Bible and looked around the room. Leaning forward with compassion in his eyes, he said, "The One who performed those miracles was sitting in the boat with the disciples, but they still didn't understand that He could provide whatever they needed. Do not focus on what you don't have or what you aren't. God will take whatever you offer Him and make it more than enough."

The story about the small boy who was with Jesus came to my mind.

> One of His disciples, Andrew . . . said to Him, "There is a lad here who has five barley loaves and two fish, but what are these for so many people?" Jesus said, "Have the people sit down." . . . Jesus then took the loaves, and having given thanks, He distributed to those who were seated; likewise also of the fish as much as they wanted. (John 6:8–11)

God spoke to my heart: *You will please Me by offering what you have and who you are. Stop hiding and trying to please everyone.*

Soon after God's revelation, I sat at my kitchen table, reading the day's devotional from *Jesus Calling*. The words were perfectly timed:

> I am pleased with you, My child. . . . You don't have to perform well in order to receive My Love. In fact, a performance focus will pull you away from Me, toward some sort of Pharisaism. This can be a subtle form of idolatry. . . . Shift your focus from your performance to My radiant Presence. The Light of My Love shines on you continually, regardless of your feelings or behavior. Your responsibility is to be receptive to this unconditional Love . . . and . . . My loving Presence.[27]

Those devotional words led to another focused prayer time. I reaffirmed to God that He matters the most to me. I asked Him to forgive my sin of caring more about what others think of my performance than I did about His unconditional approval and love. I surrendered my desire to get approval from people and asked Him again to take charge of every aspect of my life.

This principle of "spiritual breathing"—*exhaling* by confessing our sin and *inhaling* by surrendering the control of our life to Christ—brought me to repentance before God and reconnection with God's Holy Spirit.[28] As I continually apply this principle in my life, I am able to refocus my attention to God and His path and plan for me. Focusing on Him is the best safeguard against spending time and energy trying to win the approval of others.

In chapter 5, we learned that the mindset of having to create a persona is also one of the symptoms of the impostor syndrome. Clinical psychologists Dr. Joe Langford and Dr. Pauline Rose Clance present some insights on the role of therapy for those who suffer from the impostor syndrome:

> The central task of psychotherapy with impostors is to lessen the client's dependence on others' positive evaluations for his or her self-esteem and to build a more internalized sense of self-worth. . . . The goal of therapy is to make that mask no longer necessary. The metaphor of a mask recalls the writings of theorists who have believed that successful therapy helps people accept and live out of their own inner needs, as it decreases the necessity of presenting facades or images to win others' affirmation.
>
> . . . Exploration of family background will likely lead to new awarenesses of the pressures and forces within the family that led the child to adopt a role aimed at [earning approval]. This examination of the past may tap into feelings of sadness and anger. . . . The therapist can validate these feelings as the client gets in touch with the deeper needs of the self.[29]

My new perspective of focusing on God's approval instead of the approval of others instilled confidence to carry out an idea He gave me.

I belong to Word Weavers International. During our monthly meeting for Christian writers, we share success stories before dividing into small critique groups.

God prompted me to share an unusual success story. When our president, Rick, called on me, I walked to the front, carrying a notecard. "We all want to see success in whatever we're writing," I said. "If we've published a book, we look for book sales to measure our success."

Heads nodded.

"I want to tell you about a note I received from my cousin Ross. He told me that the book I'd signed and sent to him and his wife, Vanessa, arrived at their home shortly after their sweet nineteen-year-old daughter, Diana, took her life."

The group gasped.

"I cried for their deep loss. The only thing that lifted my heart were Ross's words, 'Your book helped us because you showed how you processed your grief.'" I held up the note. "Isn't this the true measure of success?"

My writer friends' responses confirmed that the message had touched their hearts. My personal victory rested on my obedience to walk into God's opportunity without knowing how they would receive my story.

Author Robert McGee says,

> We can ultimately seek either the approval of men or the approval of God as the basis of our self-worth. God wants to be the Lord of our lives, and He is unwilling to share that rightful lordship with anyone else. . . . Therefore, the only way we can overcome the fear of rejection is to *value the constant approval of God over the conditional approval of people.*[30] (Italics mine)

We can fall into the trap of thinking we need to create a persona to protect ourselves from rejection. Instead, we need to remind ourselves that God is our protector, and He accepts us unconditionally. He will help us take steps to break the stronghold of our "idol worship" of people and enable us to leave our persona behind.

Whom do you seek to please? Daily we must make our choice to look to God or look to others. When we choose to be who God created us to be, our daily walk becomes easier.

> Walk in a manner worthy of the Lord, to please Him in all respects, bearing fruit in every good work and increasing in the knowledge of God. (Colossians 1:10)

Holy Spirit, show me how to walk in a way that will please God. I want to give up trying to be who others want me to be. Help me keep my eyes on Him so I can accomplish the work He wants me to do in His power.

Reflection Questions

Chapter 9: Leaving the Persona Behind

1. Robert McGee says we can ultimately seek either the approval of men or the approval of God as the basis of our self-worth. Whose approval do you seek?

2. Your answers to the following questions may help you discover where your focus lies: What matters most to you in life? Do you find yourself encouraged or discouraged by someone else's success? Do you ever become depressed when you compare yourself or your work to someone else?

3. If you realize you are focused on gaining the approval of others, spend some time talking to God about this sin. Look at the Spiritual Breathing diagram on page 165. Apply the principle of spiritual breathing—*exhale* by confessing your sin and *inhale* by surrendering the control of your life back to Christ. This process will bring repentance before God and reconnection with God's Holy Spirit.

4. Each time you become aware that your focus for approval has shifted to people, breathe spiritually. Consider finding a prayer partner to hold you accountable.

Chapter 10
Welcoming Imperfection

Stephanie climbed the neon-lighted stairs, walked onto the glittering stage, and brought the hand mic to her mouth as the music began. With her heart engaged, words poured from her lips. She transported the audience and the judges through her musical story about a small girl abandoned by her father.

All four judges of the popular national singing competition applauded her amazing presentation. What moved me the most, though, was Stephanie's interaction with the judges.

The first judge said, "You brought my attention to the really important thing, which is the song and the story. The heart and the soul are there."

"I have to say thank you for that feedback because my head wants to sing perfectly, but the artist in my heart is [saying], 'Let me out of here!' So I feel like I did something brave today."

Another judge responded, "I applaud you for doing something scary and coming out here and laying out this passionate performance that connected to all of us."

Prior to her performance, the network had played Stephanie's video package for the audience. She told about the indelible mark her father had left on her heart when he walked away from the family. Tears came to her eyes when she added, "Maybe he'll tune into NBC, hear me sing, and say, 'That's my girl.'"

Perhaps that hope gave Stephanie the courage to ignore the strong call of perfection and let the artist in her heart come out that night. Her willingness to risk singing imperfectly opened the way for her to reveal who she really is inside.

God's love for us is never affected by how we perform. He is not looking for perfection. He's simply looking for us. Don't you suppose He enjoys our singing the most when it comes from our hearts?

God says, "I have loved you with an everlasting love; I have drawn you with unfailing kindness" (Jeremiah 31:3 NIV).

Making perfectionism our goal hinders our ability to move forward. If we never reach our goal of being a perfect artist or project manager or parent, we can feel discouraged. If we restate our goal and look for progress in those roles instead of perfection, we are empowered with energy to keep moving forward.

A memorable sign of progress in letting go of perfection became apparent in my discipleship ministry in the Philippines. I enjoyed teaching the young women, but when it came time to exchange prayer requests, I focused on their needs without revealing any of my own problems or struggles.

Things began to change through one courageous young woman in the group. Margie started saying to me week after week, "What about you? Do you need us to pray about something for you?"

Through her love and concern, Margie helped me relate to the women more personally by becoming honest and open. Instead of trying to be their perfect Bible-study leader, I began telling them how they could pray for me.

Once these precious disciples saw that I faced disappointments and challenges too, they felt more free around me. We built a closer relationship because I relaxed and let go of the need to keep up the appearance of having it all together.

In later years, back in the US, I saw additional signs of progress. I used to struggle with feelings of inferiority and impending failure every time I anticipated seeing a particular person at work. That coworker, Dean, gave an excellent performance in every arena, and I believed he expected the same of me.

When God showed me I was in bondage to perfection as a way to seek Dean's approval, I let that truth sink in. God says in John 8:31–32, "If you continue in My word, then you are truly disciples of Mine; and you will know the truth, and the truth will make you free."

One Monday morning as I drove into the beautifully landscaped grounds at our sprawling office compound, my usual dread about my coworker didn't surface.

Soon after I'd settled into my cubicle, Dean shot a question over the wall that separated our cubicles: "Hey, Gail, do you have that conference schedule ready?"

My mind spun into its usual interpretation: *He thinks I'm slow. He probably felt like saying, "Don't you have that schedule ready yet?"*

Then I changed my mind. Instead of beating myself up for inefficiency, making excuses, or making an impossible promise to him, I simply said, "I don't have it ready yet. How about noon tomorrow?"

Surprisingly he said, "Sure. Just checking."

A light turned on. Instead of interpreting people's comments from a negative point of view or believing their words contained a direct implication that I wasn't measuring up, I could assume people's words held no hidden meaning. I could respond honestly and reasonably from my own point of view and leave the results of their response to God.

Something else clicked inside me. Previously, I'd spent each working day focused on my performance without caring how Dean was doing. I needed to change that.

"Hey, how was your weekend?" I asked.

"Great. Our family went to the beach."

"Fun. Wondering how things are going for your board presentation tomorrow?"

"Good. Thanks for asking."

"Hope it's a huge success."

My new perspective normalized our relationship and made me feel more connected to him as a coworker and friend.

Brené Brown wrote an intriguing book called *The Gifts of Imperfection: Let Go of Who You Think You're Supposed to Be and Embrace Who You Are.* During a decade of research, she conducted extensive surveys to determine how the universal experiences of shame and fear affect us. Brené saw three "gifts" emerge in the lives of those who embraced imperfection: courage, compassion, and connection. She believes these gifts can become tools for developing our worthiness by helping us slowly let go of the fear that holds us back.

Brené says:

> If we want to fully experience love and belonging, we must believe that we are *worthy* of love and belonging. . . .
>
> When we can let go of what other people think and own our story, we gain access to our worthiness—the feeling that we are enough just as we are and that we are worthy of love and belonging. When we spend a lifetime trying to distance ourselves from the parts of our lives that don't fit with who we think we're supposed to be, we stand outside of our story and hustle for our worthiness by

constantly performing, perfecting, pleasing, and proving.[31]

After capturing the importance of welcoming imperfection, I started experiencing the gifts Brené Brown pointed out. My new *courage* to admit who I am, including my weaknesses, has created a deeper *compassion* for other people and their personal life situations. This compassion has led to valuable and rewarding *connections*.

My relationships are stronger and deeper. These authentic relationships have allowed me to experience a clearer sense of love and belonging.

God continually brings people across my path who are willing to reveal deep, troubling, and heartbreaking circumstances. He gives me compassion for them and provides wisdom for saying whatever will make a difference in their day or their future decisions. God is filling me with more joy and confidence in ministering to others.

Some of my close friends have sought counseling and individualized personal therapy to keep them moving toward open and authentic relationships. The discoveries one friend has made inspired me to keep refuting the false belief that we have to be perfect for people to accept us:

> You and I are perfectionists. We are the types who would want our house sparkling before our house cleaner comes. We want to become models of emotional stability before we seek help from professionals who can help us deal with our internal stories that say we are not good enough, or that we will never make it, or that we have no future.

Before I met with my therapist, I had written my experiences during the last twenty years. His email response, after reading my long journal, was, "I feel you are ready *enough* to take the next step, so I would be happy to set up a phone appointment with you."

That word "enough" made such a difference for me. I realized this is "one party I don't have to dress up for." I could and should come as I am. I don't have to heal myself before I come for healing. From his perspective, I was ready *enough*.

This new way of thinking helps me accept that I can't do it all. It also shows me ways to do what I am ready to do, one small step at a time. Those small steps are surprisingly scary sometimes. Yet a part of me says, "Let's get this show on the road!"

I want to engage in a footrace to get to where God wants me to be. I'm learning that how I get there is not as important as getting there. To me, this concept drips with hope, and even though I am cautious and untrusting at times, I am "ready enough" to walk one more mile.

When we let go of perfection and become willing to welcome our imperfections, we set ourselves free. We're not expecting perfection of ourselves, and we stop expecting others to be perfect. Our personal time with people is more enjoyable because we are not wasting our energy trying to be perfect in their eyes.

Are you less inclined to seek perfection from yourself now? You will enjoy life more.

But he said to me, "My grace is sufficient for you, for my power is made perfect in weakness." Therefore I will boost all the more gladly about my weaknesses, so that Christ's power may rest on me. (2 Corinthians 12:9 NIV)

Jesus, thank You for Your power, which overcomes my weaknesses. I don't need to hide my imperfections or failures. I can be grateful for them because they reflect Your power in me.

We are on a journey that is taking us closer to becoming the real person we are. To help us make progress, we talked about the devastating results of "Living in Captivity." Identifying and acknowledging our chosen strategies that have kept us in bondage were important steps to take.

Then we focused on "Breaking Strongholds" that deceive us into believing we need to stay in our prisons. Step by step, through God's power, we are pushing through those barriers.

Remember this truth:

In God's strength, people who struggle with the fear of rejection can walk out of their self-made prisons and taste the freedom that will allow them to become who God made them to be.

Reflection Questions

Chapter 10: Welcoming Imperfection

1. Have you seen progress in letting go of perfection and welcoming imperfection? In what ways has your growth in this area reduced the stress you previously experienced while trying to reach perfection?

2. What changes have you seen in your life inside or outside of your home since your decision?

3. What differences have you observed in your relationship with friends? Do you find yourself more willing to talk about your disappointments or struggles?

4. Have the changes in your life led to more opportunities to sit and talk about life with close friends and new friends? If you are not the sit-and-talk type of person, do you see other signs that indicate your friends are more comfortable around you?

5. Have you noticed the three gifts of courage, compassion, and connection emerging in your life? Give some examples.

6. Now that you have finished the chapters in "Breaking Strongholds" and considered your answers to the Reflection Questions, do you have any additional discoveries or experiences you want to record in the Journal Your Journey section (pages 160–162) or on your computer or mobile device? Question 3 of the Reflection Questions for chapter 15 includes some suggested questions to consider.

Part Three
Tasting Freedom

Chapter 11
Embracing the Present

"I have a reverse rejection story to tell you," Brent said from across the table at brunch. His wife, Karen, had brought up the topic of the book I'd been writing on the fear of rejection.

"I want to hear your story, Brent."

He set down his coffee cup and drew a deep breath. "As early as I can remember, my parents told me I was special because I was adopted. I never felt insecure or experienced a need to search for my birth parents to receive validation or fill a hole that only my birth parents could fill. My parents were the best. I had a wonderful childhood in a loving family who taught me about God. They were always willing for me to find my birth parents if that was important to me."

Karen turned to Brent. "So helpful that they were open to that."

"It did help. And my birthday has always been special for me because that was the one day of the year my birth mom would think of me. As I got older, I grew more curious about my birth parents. I made a half-hearted attempt to look for my birth mother a few times, to no avail."

"Isn't it hard to find adoptive parents?" I asked.

"I knew the laws had changed, and it had become easier to locate birth parents of sealed adoptions. I could hire a private investigator, but that seemed like cheating. I needed to do the work myself. As I approached fifty, I wondered if my mom and birth mom would ever meet."

I thought about that as our waitress set bagels and fruit before us. "That's true. Perhaps time was running out."

"I was afraid so too," Brent said. "So at 3:30 one morning, I started searching. After discovering a state adoption directory, I entered my information. A few minutes later, a woman in Chicago emailed back: 'I can help you.' She explained she liked being an angel who helped put together reunions. She asked for more information. By 6 a.m., she had found my birth mom and included the name, address, and phone number."

Brent's eyes glistened, as if he treasured the memory of the angel finding his birth mother. "After fifty years of wondering, within a couple of hours the answers filled my screen. I asked myself, *Now what do I do?* A plan formed in my mind."

"The possible outcomes of his plan made me a bit nervous," Karen said as she shifted in her seat, "but I wanted to support Brent."

He gave her a quick look that communicated his appreciation. "The week before my birthday, I handwrote a letter: 'I've been looking forward to writing you for many, many years. I believe you may be my birth mom.' I told her my birthday, the hospital I was born in, and details about her life, which I had learned from the adoption agency. Then I said, 'I'm thankful for you and the life you gave me. I grew up in a loving Christian family. My wife and our two boys are my joy. I am indeed blessed. I plan to call you on my fiftieth birthday. I want to say thank you.'"

After taking a sip of my coffee, I asked, "Did you have the courage to mail your letter?"

"Yes. And when my birthday arrived, I made the call. Unfortunately, I had to leave a message on her answering machine. After recovering a bit, Karen and I drove to a restaurant for my birthday lunch. On the way, we stopped at the post office.

"In our box waited a birthday card from my birth mom. What a joy! The front of the card said, 'Have a Blessed Birthday.' Inside were a few personal words from her. She explained she would be traveling on my birthday, so she wouldn't be home to answer my call. Also, inside was a picture of her with her brothers and their children—new uncles, aunts, and cousins for me."

Karen leaned toward me. "We were both shocked. I sat there in awe that his mother had expressed this kind of love to Brent, even before she met him."

"I admit I choked up as I opened that card." With a husky voice, he continued. "After she returned from her trip, we talked by phone. It was a comfortable conversation, almost as if we had talked before. I think we were both amazed and excited to hear each other's voices after all those years.

"Before we hung up, we set a time to meet later that summer. I wondered about our first meeting and how it would go. When I saw her, though, I quickly forgot any worry about how I should act. I smiled and enjoyed the matter-of-fact way we said hello."

I had moved closer to make sure I caught every word. "Brent, I can't even imagine how you felt to see her for the first time after fifty years. No wonder you were anxious. Seems as if you both forgot your worries once you saw each other."

"Right. We embraced as mother and son. This was something I'd dreamed about my whole life. We talked as though we had known each other for years and yet had so much to share."

"Did she tell you about her family?" I said, pushing away the food that had suddenly become much less interesting than my friend's story.

"I learned she had grown up with her brothers on the small family farm and stayed there through college. As soon as she graduated, she moved to a different town to begin her career. After she got settled, she discovered she was pregnant. Her roommate was the only person who knew."

"She didn't tell her parents?"

"No, and she never told the baby's father, either. Also, she waited to invite her family and friends to visit her until well after I was born. Eventually she married, but didn't have any other children."

He paused, as if to let the poignancy sweep through us before he went on.

"She said she always thought I would be mad at her for giving me up. Apparently, she envisioned me coming to the door, yelling at her."

Karen shook her head. "If she'd known you, she never would have thought that."

"Her statement shook me. I assured her I was grateful for what she did, because it gave me such a happy life. I had loving parents and a wonderful childhood. Now I have a beautiful family life with Karen and my boys and a fulfilling job. I told her that my only intent in writing the letter was to thank her."

"Did your mother ever tell her family about you?"

"It took six months. She sent all her relatives a group email, saying, 'I have a son.'"

"Wow! That must have been a shock to them."

"I'm sure it was. Fortunately, all of them have extended grace and acceptance to us. I think she has enjoyed sharing Karen and me with her extended family during the past few years."

"What was your own family's response?"

A little line appeared between Karen's brows. "While the real story is beautiful, especially the conclusion, we didn't escape a certain amount of tension and apprehension. We were opening ourselves up to something new."

Brent explained, "There were a lot of emotions because we were bringing someone new into the family. Some in the family are excited. But I can sense some of them wondering what this will do to our family dynamics."

"Have your two mothers had a chance to meet?"

"Not yet. Maybe someday, but my mother is eighty-eight years old, and her health is my priority." Brent cut open his bagel and slathered cream cheese on it.

"I'm thankful for the gift of life God gave me through my adoption. I'm humbled that my parents loved me so well. I'm also grateful for this chance to know my birth mom. Our separate lives have come full circle."

"Such a touching story, Brent. You extended grace to a woman who thought you would hate her. That reunion changed your mother's life forever."

Brent's smile reflected an array of emotions, including intense joy that has spread to many people because he embraced his present life rather than dwelling in the past.

He could have become bitter when his parents told him he was adopted. He could have felt unloved and abandoned all those years. He could have nurtured an unforgiving heart toward his birth mother and let the fact he was adopted define who he is as a person.

At age fifty, Bob chose to embrace the present by extending the gift of grace to the mother who'd given him up. When he did, she opened her heart and revealed her lifelong secret. That led to the freedom to celebrate the birth—and rebirth—of her son. Brent set his birth mother free to let go of her fear of rejection by her son and welcome him into her present life.

Their past remains. Their memories endure, tucked inside their hearts. Yet the memories they have created in the three years since their reunion have overpowered the past. Now they both live new lives because of grace.

Sometimes we allow memories and past experiences to define us and hold us back from experiencing freedom in the present. When we bring buried memories out of the darkness and expose them to light, we can release those memories to God. He gives us courage to let go.

Opportunities to fear will crop up, even after we step on the path of freedom. Fear about the responsibilities of today. Fear about our inadequacy for tomorrow. Fear about how things might turn out in the future.

Our response in those moments of testing is crucial. We can let fear rule us, as it has in the past, or we can choose to trust God to help us move past our fear that day.

Form the habit of turning to God's Word and claiming promises of His presence, deliverance, and protection, expressed in verses like these:

> Have mercy on me, my God, have mercy on me, for in you I take refuge. I will take refuge in the shadow of your wings until the disaster has passed. (Psalm 57:1 NIV)

> Be strong and courageous, do not be afraid or tremble at them, for the Lord your God is the one

who goes with you. He will not fail you or forsake you. (Deuteronomy 31:6)

Because he has loved Me, therefore I will deliver him; I will set him securely on high, because he has known My name. He will call upon Me, and I will answer him; I will be with him in trouble; I will rescue him and honor him. With a long life I will satisfy him and let him see My salvation. (Psalm 91:14–16)

But as for me, I will watch expectantly for the Lord; I will wait for the God of my salvation. My God will hear me. Do not rejoice over me, O my enemy. Though I fall I will rise; though I dwell in darkness, the Lord is a light for me. (Micah 7:7–8)

Brené Brown painted a picture of freedom that depicts the kind of person I want to be as I embrace my present life, abandoned to the moment. She wrote:

The Hopi Indians have a saying, "To watch us dance is to hear our hearts speak." I know how much courage it takes to let people hear our hearts speak, but life is way too precious to spend it pretending like we're super-cool and totally in control when we could be laughing, singing, and dancing.[32]

Hold on to life's moments. Jesus died for you so you could be free to live and laugh and build new memories.

Do you sometimes let memories and experiences hinder you? Give them to God so you can be free to embrace the freedom of today. Don't miss the opportunity.

WILL THE REAL PERSON PLEASE STAND UP?

The thief comes only to steal and kill and destroy;
I came that they may have life, and have it abundantly. (John 10:10)

*Jesus, thank You for dying for me so I could experience an abun-
dant life. Prevent me from becoming absorbed by what has happened
in the past and giving the enemy any chance to defeat me. Help me
celebrate today by giving thanks.*

Reflection Questions

Chapter 11: Embracing the Present

1. What emotions rose to the surface as you read Brent's story? What impressed you the most about his choice and ability to embrace the present?

2. Has someone extended grace to you in a way that helped you let go of a certain situation you were struggling with? Explain.

3. Have you been able to bring a buried memory out of the darkness and ask God to shed His light on it? What new understanding do you have about that memory? What difference has that made for you?

4. Review the verses near the end of this chapter that promise God's presence, deliverance, and protection. Which verse encouraged you the most? Consider posting that one, or a favorite verse, on your computer or writing it on a notecard to keep in a prominent place.

5. Give an example of one way you embraced life today without thinking of the past or focusing on your future.

6. As you begin this new section, "Tasting Freedom," keep in mind new discoveries and experiences you will want to record in the Journal Your Journey section (pages 160–162) or on your computer or mobile device as you finish each chapter.

Chapter 12

Climbing the Mountain

Not many of us are living at our best. We linger in the lowlands because we are afraid to climb into the mountains. The steepness and ruggedness dismay us—and so we stay in the misty valleys and do not learn the mystery of the hills. We do not know what we lose in our self-indulgence. We do not know what glory awaits us, if only we had courage for the mountain climb, what blessing we should find, if only we would move to the uplands of God!

—J.R. Miller
Unto the Hills!: A Meditation on Psalm 121

Many times we're afraid to climb real mountains. In our daily lives, we might be overwhelmed when we see a "mountain" looming in front of us.

Some mountain climbers thrive on the thrill of reaching for the top. Here is the story of one of them, which was captured by The 700 Club:

> Brian Dickinson is a highly skilled and self-sufficient mountain climber. He has summitted many of the world's tallest peaks. But in 2011, at the top of Mount Everest, his survival was beyond his ability and control. . . .

Brian's intense physical training had him ready, but nothing can prepare a climber for the death zone on Everest. . . . He began his climb with his friend Dennis and their Sherpas, the local mountain guides. But shortly into their climb Dennis became ill and stayed behind. Brian and his Sherpa continued the ascent. Issues arose the next day. . . .

At 26,000 feet, Brian and his Sherpa, Pasang, rested. At nightfall they made their summit attempt. But just 1000 feet short of the top, Pasang became ill leaving Brian with a tough decision to make. [He continued on. Afterward, he revealed that during the whole time without his Sherpa, he felt a Presence that assured him he was not alone.]

Brian climbed through the night. The next day, he made it to the top of Mount Everest, the highest point on earth. [He experienced moments of pride mixed with exhaustion. Eager to return to his family after a long time apart, he turned to go down the mountain, still attached to his rope. Then, without warning, he went snow blind.]

He pressed on. But things went from bad to worse. [His mask started sucking into his face, and he ripped it off, causing damage to his eyes. The oxygen tank that Pasang left with him stopped working. Brian tried taking deep breaths of the thin air, but nothing came in.]

[He dropped to his knees and prayed a simple prayer: "God, I can't do this alone. Please help me."]

On the other side of the world, friends and family were suddenly compelled to pray for Brian. . . .

[He said he witnessed a miracle. At his moment of surrender, he felt God lift him up by the back of his down suit. He stood and felt strong. Unexplained energy and hope entered his body.]

Then Brian tried Pasang's oxygen tank again. This time it worked. He made it down to their camp at 26,000 feet where Pasang was waiting for him. . . .

With the help of Pasang and Dennis, Brian made it the rest of the way down Everest and home to his family. One month later his sight returned to normal. Brian says he is thankful God was with him every step of the way to the top of the world, and back down again. . . .

Brian concludes, ". . .God is always there. He'll lead you through the toughest times and help you survive the impossible."[33]

What mountains loom before you right now? Most likely you're not attempting Mount Everest, but you might have some tough, seemingly impossible challenges in front of you. Even though we walk in greater freedom now, we can't live in a bubble of unreality. Reality will sprinkle and even drench us with unexpected difficulties and delays.

Sometimes a crisis moment will crash into our lives, changing us forever. In her article "When Loving Is Not Easy," my friend Jo Lodevico Lee describes the life-altering mountain she and her husband never expected to climb:

> I woke up to a nightmare on the early morning of November 17 last year with the sight of my husband Steinar crawling on our apartment floor to go to the bathroom. Despite my support and a cane, this guy—who has hiked countless mountains on

rugged terrains—couldn't stand, let alone walk. In shock over this surreal scene, I stood still, unable to move myself, until I heard him say, "Call 911."

He was rushed to the hospital and thrust into an unexpected ordeal. For the next three weeks, he endured myriad diagnostic tests . . . as more than a dozen specialists tried to figure out the cause of his paralysis. He suffered sleepless nights, tormented by physical pain and the anguish of uncertainty. Sleeping aids and strong painkillers hardly helped. If anything, their side effects only increased his distress.

By God's grace, at the end of those three long weeks, he heard the name of that which invaded his body and our lives: Guillain-Barre Syndrome (GBS), a condition so rare only one person among 100,000 develops it.

Today Steinar undergoes physical and occupational therapies as part of his recovery. He can walk only a short distance before he gets fatigued. Sometimes he walks like a penguin, and most times, gingerly, like a child just learning to take his first steps. His neurologist reminds him to be patient with his recovery as his body has suffered so much trauma, and that on average, those afflicted with GBS take between six months to one year to recover fully. . . .

The Lord has provided us with family and friends who have come alongside us to help us survive during Steinar's ordeal. On different occasions, my sister-in-law, her husband, and my brother-in-law flew from out of state and granted me reprieve from caring for Steinar 24/7. . . .

The first time Steinar walked the same distance he crawled on that unforgettable morning,

I wanted to cry. I remembered those early times when I'd beg the Lord to wake me and Steinar up from the nightmare of his paralysis. Seeing him stand and walk on his own these days makes me grateful that we're out of that nightmare—one that actually gave me space to have and to hold my husband in sickness and in health. [34]

With God, we always have hope for a solution, a breakthrough, a small light shining on our darkest moments. God's presence is most evident during the darkest, hopeless times.

Uncertainty can cause our fear to loom heavier over us. But inviting our fear into our lives and letting it walk through our days of mountain climbing can lessen its power until we conquer higher and higher peaks in God's strength.

My friend Pat reminded me of her favorite verse about fear: "So do not fear, for I am with you; do not be dismayed, for I am your God. I will strengthen you and help you; I will uphold you with my righteous right hand" (Isaiah 41:10 NIV). She added her own significant conclusion: "I came to realize I show love to the Lord when I say no to fears and yes to trust."

We can't fight fear in our own strength. God knows we need His power, His weapons, to stand strong and not give in to our fears or the schemes of the enemy. The enemy of God is like a mighty roaring lion who roams around, waiting for a chance to devour us.[35]

I remember a particular day when fear threatened to overcome me. God painted this scene in my mind so vividly that I felt compelled to put my experience into words:

Untying the Ropes

Fear crept in quietly,
Seeking a shadowy corner,
A place to observe my moves
And detect my intentions.

As I stepped out in faith that day,
Confidently following God's direction,
Fear knew there was no place for him;
He was doomed to stay in darkness.

Then I anxiously looked around me
Wondering, *What if this happens . . .*
Suddenly a siren went off.
Fear leapt from the shadows,
tying ropes around me,
deepening my anxiety,
dimming my hope of rescue.

As I stood there immobilized by Fear,
I cried,
"Where is my hope?
Who will set me free?"

Suddenly You were in front of me.
As I watched,
You untied my ropes,
melted my anxious thoughts,
renewed my hope.

Once again,
You took my hand
And helped me walk away from Fear.

gp 1994

126

Fear takes advantage of every sliver of possibility of tying us up. Fear of rejection dredges up memories, trapping us in yesterday's experiences. Fear causes us to shrink back from pressured circumstances of today and the "what ifs" of tomorrow.

Lysa TerKeurst, author of *Uninvited,* says:

> The enemy loves to take our rejection and twist it into a raw, irrational fear that God really doesn't have a good plan for us. [This fear] replaces the truths we've trusted with hopeless lies. Satan knows what consumes us, controls us. Therefore, the more consumed we are with rejection, the more he can control our emotions, our thinking, and our actions.[36]

Spiritual battles rage every day. Building fear in us is one of the enemy's strategies. Fear renders us powerless and instills hopelessness in us. We must take the battle seriously and cling to Him in trust if we are to walk forward in freedom and climb the mountain ahead of us.

Ephesians 6:11 reminds us, "Put on the full armor of God, so that you will be able to stand firm against the schemes of the devil." When we put on God's "full armor" by praying about and naming each part of the armor aloud—helmet of salvation, breastplate of righteousness, belt of truth, shoes of the preparation of the gospel of peace, sword of the Spirit, and the shield of faith—we are able to "stand firm" against the enemy.

In the midst of the battle, God promises to fight for us. Our responsibility is to focus on Him.

> Therefore, since we have so great a cloud of witnesses surrounding us, let us also lay aside every

encumbrance and the sin which so easily entangles us, and let us run with endurance the race that is set before us, fixing our eyes on Jesus, the author and perfecter of faith, who for the joy set before Him endured the cross, despising the shame, and has sat down at the right hand of the throne of God. (Hebrews 12:1–2)

We all will have mountains to climb. That is part of life. Sometimes our footsteps may be slow and unsteady. At other times we push ahead, making great process as we weave our way upward.

In the midst of disappointments, heartaches, and sorrows along the way, God will comfort us and beckon us to rest a while on the side of the path.

While there, He restores our energy so we can stand again and run our race with endurance. By faith, we will make it to the top of the mountain because our hand is secure in His.

The steps of a man are established by the Lord, and He delights in his way. When he falls, he will not be hurled headlong, because the Lord is the One who holds his hand. (Psalm 37:23–24)

Father, thank You that whenever I stumble, weighed down by the day's burden, You pick me up and restore my strength, so together we can climb to the top of the mountain.

Reflection Questions

Chapter 12: Climbing the Mountain

1. Describe what impacted you the most when you read about Brian Dickinson's experiences on Mount Everest.

2. What were your thoughts when you read the devastating news about Steinar's rare condition? Have you or any family members faced uncertain medical situations in the past? In what ways did God help you deal with your fears and hang on to hope?

3. Are you climbing any "mountains" right now? Describe your situation and what you are trusting God to do for you.

4. Do you put on the armor of God as protection against the enemy, as explained in Ephesians 6? In what way does that affect your mindset each day?

Chapter 13

Enjoying the View

Beth Moore says, "We tend to unweave rainbows instead of beholding them. Behold the moment."[37]

Perhaps analytical people like me try to unweave rainbows. We try to make sense out of things we see rather than simply beholding what God created for us to enjoy.

I remember one particular rainbow captured on camera by Richard, the best friend of my brother Greig. Richard and I happened to have been in Folly Beach, South Carolina, on the same day because we were switching places. He and I had become a tight team of caregivers for Greig, who was hospitalized with leukemia.

After visiting Greig at the hospital, we dashed into a grocery store before driving to the condo, our temporary headquarters each time one of us was on duty. Greig had been in the hospital for more than three months following a relapse after a bone marrow transplant. A courageous fighter, he kept going in hopes that his condition would stabilize. We, too, tried to stay positive that he would win his battle.

As we dodged rain puddles in the parking lot on the way to the car that day, I spotted a rainbow. "Oh, Richard, look. Please take a picture of me in front of it."

I wanted to preserve that moment. The rainbow that spread across the sky painted hope in my heart for Greig's recovery. God declared that a rainbow in the clouds on a rainy day would always be a symbol of His covenant to take care of us.[38]

Those beautiful colors became for me an embrace from God in the darkest time of my life. I was not alone. He was there with me.

God reminded me of His presence on countless days after that, including the moment the phone rang with news for my niece Regan and me that her beloved father and my brother had died. Our hearts broke as we cried together, but we both clung to God, our lifeline. We cherished the time we had sat at his bedside only a few hours before.

Greig enjoys endless rainbows now, along with all the other beauty God has created for him in heaven. I'll still keep looking for rainbows here on earth, each one God's unique display at the very moment I need it.

It's all about perspective, isn't it?

I could have glanced at the rainbow, quickly climbed into Richard's car, and nursed a heavy heart on the way back to the condo. Instead, I admired that rainbow in the sky and remembered God's promise to be with me always. My viewpoint changed. So did my heart.

The way we view our daily lives makes a difference.

- View from the kitchen: Are we grateful for our home, or do we complain about our daily chores?
- View from our backyard: Do we see the beauty of the trees and flowers, or do we see the garden that needs tending and the grass that needs mowing?
- View during a walk in the neighborhood: Do we notice the scenery and the people, or do we let boredom creep in?

- View from the hillside: Do we relish the chance to get out of the city, or do our minds keep flitting to that next thing on our to-do list?
- View of an important decision: Do we rely on God to show us what to do, or do we still wonder how we're going to conquer this mountain alone?
- View from a hospital room: Do we let God's presence flood our heavy hearts, or do we give in to despair and hopelessness and leave God out?
- View from the boardroom: Do we believe God will give us the confidence and wisdom we need, or are we afraid our presentations won't be well received?

It's also crucial to consider how we view ourselves. In their book *Nothing to Prove*, David and Caron Loveless present helpful questions:

1. If you remove . . .
   Your job
   Your roles
   Your gender
   Your relationships
   Your titles
   Your possessions
   Your degrees
   Your achievements
   Your failures . . .

Who do you say that you are?

2. Without naming . . .
   Your family
   The work you do
   Things you own
   A role you play in a primary relationship . . .

   How would you describe yourself to someone you've just met?

3. Who you truly think you are at your core will influence every decision and every reaction to every loss and every gain you ever will have . . .

   When you're alone and no one's looking, who do you really think you are? [39]

This exercise may have brought us some "aha" moments when we discovered what we think our personal identity is.

Pastor Jessica LaGrone says in her Bible study called *Namesake*, "[Your] new identity . . . can come only from knowing the One who created you, the One who knew you before anyone else. Knowing the great I AM has changed who I am. God's revelation of who He is has brought about transformation in my own life."[40]

How can we know more about God? Discovering His many attributes,[41] like love, compassion, justice, mercy, and faithfulness, helps us learn new facets about His character. However, we cannot fully experience who He is until we allow Him to be in our lives and control our days.

Throughout my childhood and young adulthood years, I learned about God and His love for me. I loved Him, prayed, read my Bible, and went to church. From my perspective, God lived in heaven and I lived on earth. I spent my days trying to please Him through my words, thoughts, and actions.

During my sophomore year in college, a friend told me about an upcoming Christian student meeting on campus. When the day arrived, I joined my friend at the meeting place. The speaker related things familiar to me until he said, "God wants us to know Him personally through having a relationship with Him."

A personal relationship with God? That's a dimension of life I'm not experiencing. I want this.

That night changed my life. The teacher led us in a prayer in which I confessed my sins that had kept me separated from Him, thanked Christ for dying on the cross for my sins, and asked Him to come into my heart and life. Because of His promise, I believed Christ heard my prayer and came into my life when I invited Him. He also promised to stay in my life forever.

Have you discovered this relationship for yourself? Perhaps you made that decision many years ago. Maybe it was in more recent years. Possibly you haven't yet heard about this awesome opportunity to know God personally.

The Bible says God loves us with unconditional love. We don't have to measure up. We don't have to earn His approval. We don't have to try to change our ways before we say yes to His invitation to know Him personally. Jesus Christ's death provided a way for us to begin our personal relationship with God.

If you haven't made that decision yet and would like to, you can say a simple prayer like the one below or pray in your own words. God will hear your prayer.

God, I want to have a personal relationship with You.
I have lived separated from You because of my sins.
Thank You that Your Son, Jesus, died to pay for all
my sins—past, present, and future. I invite Jesus to
come into my life as my Savior and Lord. Thank You
for forgiving my sins, coming into my life, and giving
me eternal life so I can live with You forever. Help
me become the person You created me to be. In Jesus's
name. Amen.

God gives us a new identity when we begin a relationship with Him. He created us and designed us the way He wants us to be. From His viewpoint, His design of us is perfect. Psalm 139 presents a beautiful description:

> For you created my inmost being;
>> you knit me together in my mother's womb.
> I praise you because I am fearfully and wonderfully made;
>> your works are wonderful,
>> I know that full well.
> My frame was not hidden from you
>> when I was made in the secret place,
>> when I was woven together in the depths of the earth.
> Your eyes saw my unformed body;
>> all the days ordained for me were written in your book
>> before one of them came to be. (Psalm 139:13–16 NIV)

God wants to transform us from the fearful person we used to be into a confident person who is free to enjoy each day. We can live with the peace, security, love, and acceptance that only God can give us.

Lysa TerKeurst says:

> Old patterns of thought must be torn out, and a new way of looking at the core of who I am using God's truth has to be put into place. My identity must be anchored to the truth of who God is and who He is to me. Only then can I find a stability beyond what my feelings will ever allow. The closer I align my truth with His truth, the more closely I identify with God—and the more my identity really is in Him.
>
> . . . When my identity is tied to circumstances I become extremely insecure because circumstances are unpredictable and ever-changing.
>
> The exhausting manipulation and control it takes to protect an identity based on circumstances will crush our hearts and hide the best of who we are behind a wall of insecurity.
>
> . . . We must tie our identities to our unchanging, unflinching, unyielding, undeniably good, and unquestionably loving God. And the ties that truly bind me to Him and the truth of who I am in Him are given to me in those quiet moments where I say, "I'm Yours, God."[42]

Viewpoint is important because it affects the way we look at life. Do we make the most of every moment?

Our view of ourselves can easily be marred if we try to be someone we are not. Are we still tempted? We no longer need to be swayed by our circumstances or people's feedback. As those who belong to God, we can be secure in who we are.

Most important is our view of God. When we have a personal relationship with Him, everything changes. We are transformed into new people with a growing dependence on God. Confirming this truth is 2 Corinthians 5:17: "Therefore if anyone is in Christ, he is a new creature; the old things passed away; behold, new things have come."

Our new identity is wrapped up in who He is because His life is in us.

As the days pass by, we can depend on God to help people see more and more of Him in us. That's the best view they can have.

> God sees not as man sees, for man looks at the outward appearance, but the Lord looks at the heart. (1 Samuel 16:7)

Jesus, thank You for changing the way I view myself. I belong to You now, and that's who I am. Keep my heart steady and focused on what You say about me. Remind me to let You control my life.

Reflection Questions

Chapter 13: Enjoying the View

1. Describe the way you tend to view your daily life. Explain if you are generally satisfied, or describe a change you would like to make in your thinking.

2. What is your response to the statement, "Your new identity can come only from knowing the One who created you"?

3. Have you had a chance to begin a personal relationship with God?

4. If so, when did that happen? Describe what led you to accept Christ into your heart and a specific difference Christ has made in your life.

5. If you haven't begun a personal relationship with God, what do you think is holding you back? Would you like to accept His invitation and begin your new relationship with Him today? You can use the prayer in this chapter (page 136) or pray in your own words.

6. Reread Psalm 139. What is your response to the fact that God created you and designed you the way He desired? How do you think this relates to your personal identity?

7. On page 137, reread what Lysa TerKeurst says about the negative effects of anchoring our identity to our circumstances rather than to God. In your own words, describe what can happen if we base our identity on circumstances.

Chapter 14
Anticipating the Future

I don't like change. I prefer predictability. My decision at a recent crossroads, however, thrust me into unchartered territory.

After I entered my senior years, friends began posing the question, "Gail, any plans for retirement?"

My answer remained the same: "No. Too many exciting things going on right now."

I was serving on the leadership team of The Significance Project of Campus Crusade/Cru. Its focus is to create resources to help Christians around the world learn who God created them to be and to do what He is calling them to do as they multiply disciples.

This assignment fit perfectly with my love for writing and teaching. My role also capitalized on my strength of administration to meet the needs of my team and help those in other countries who wanted to translate, print, and distribute the resources we created.

Everything changed one summer day in 2016. God asked me to let go of my ministry with Campus Crusade/Cru and step into a new journey of ministering in the Orlando community.

I was shocked with God's directive and dialogued with Him. "Could You tell me more, Lord?"

I want you to refocus your life.

I prayed about this prospective change for a long time, because it would mean letting go of my ministry with Campus Crusade that I had enjoyed for fifty years. I'd be leaving a position I was comfortable with and from which I derived a lot of meaning and significance. At the large headquarters where I served, longtime friends and coworkers loved and accepted me. I had flourished in that environment.

Stepping into my own ministry, which I would create, brought with it some hesitation and questions. Would my tendency toward fear of rejection hinder me? Would people accept me as a solo act in the same way they had when I worked with Campus Crusade?

"God, I am willing to take this step of faith, but how will it be possible to leave my job? Who will take my place?"

My job was intertwined with every aspect of The Significance Project. It seemed an impossible task to disengage myself and find people to replace me.

God began supplying my need. He prompted two new women to join our team. As my director and I talked, we realized they could each learn major aspects of my job.

Then came the huge responsibility of training these women, finishing or passing on all the pending projects I'd started, and organizing all my files for others to use.

I had to deal with the sadness of leaving my team, other co-workers, and friends at the Cru headquarters. Thankfully, I was not moving out of town, so I didn't need to say goodbye.

While working hard to finish well at Cru, I experienced God's confidence about what lay ahead. His peace enabled me to anticipate my future with joy.

The main reason I said yes to God's directive and moved ahead was His assurance that this new plan would give me more time to fulfill the personal mission He had given me: "Through writing, teaching, and speaking, to help others know God and live for Him."

Through fifty years of spiritual growth and growing closer to God, I was able to recognize that God's mission for me embraced the passion of my heart. The mission I would now be able to live out more fully represented the real me. It was time to let people see the person I had become.

One year later, at our US Staff Conference, I celebrated the privilege I'd had to work for fifty years with this incredible international Christian organization that serves in 191 countries. They have provided resources that paved the way for millions to come to know Christ personally, as well as resources for training believers to become multiplying disciples.[43]

My transition into ministering full time in Orlando was relatively smooth because I was already involved in writing, teaching, and speaking. Now I could minister in those ways full time. My personal relationship with God and the fifty years of training and nurturing from Cru had prepared me for this season of my life.

While putting things in motion for this transition, I noticed how God overpowered my fear of rejection. I could have asked myself the usual fear-based questions: *What will my team think? What will other staff members say? Am I capable of walking into this new avenue of ministry?*

Instead, God gave me faith to trust His plan and to release my need to know what people might think. I also surrendered the need to know all the details ahead of time. It is a process, but I'm learning to let go more frequently. This change of mind has helped me step into this new season with more confidence and freedom to be myself.

Paul Richardson says,

> God's voice always moves us in the direction of freedom. . . . To taste of this freedom, we must make a life habit of letting go. Along the winding, fluctuating paths into the future, we must be quick to say "Release!" . . . Could it be that our greatest barriers to freedom are our own heart addictions—

the synthetic elements that substitute God? Our possessions, heart addictions, and our compulsive needs can enslave us—or they can be released forever, setting us free to truly live in the freedom of the Spirit.[44]

God wants us to be free. He surrendered His Son to bring about our freedom. Sometimes we resist, holding back from taking a leap into freedom because we're worried we won't survive. We look at our weaknesses lying side by side with our strengths and question whether we will succeed in this new venture. "What ifs" loom in our future, but we don't know how things will turn out.

God says, "Nothing is impossible with Me.[45] Don't look at what you think you are capable of doing; look at what I can do when you're connected to Me."

> Abide in Me, and I in you. As the branch cannot bear fruit of itself unless it abides in the vine, so neither can you unless you abide in Me. I am the vine, you are the branches; he who abides in Me and I in him, he bears much fruit, for apart from Me you can do nothing. (John 15:4–5)

When God directs us to a different path, it usually involves unfamiliar territory. In our time of need, He promises to be the Vine that will nourish us so He can freely produce fruit in and through us.

He wants us to take off our masks, come out of hiding, and allow people to know the person He created us to be. Once we are willing to reveal the real us and people compare it to who we were before, we become proof that God can overpower and overcome anything that has happened to us in the past. He wants to make something beautiful of our lives.

One of my friends said, "Don't shrink back from enjoying your new freedom. God is delighted to showcase you because it highlights His power in your life."

Always we're faced with the daily choice of either depending on ourselves or depending on God's Spirit. We can choose to rely on the Holy Spirit to help us rise above the fear of rejection. We can live as people who are loved and empowered to be the person God created us to be.

For the mind set on the flesh is death, but the mind set on the Spirit is life and peace. (Romans 8:6)

Lysa TerKeurst imagined this interaction with God:

God: "It's not about you *becoming* anything. Your soul was made to simply *be* with Me. And the more you are with Me, the more you will stop fearing what the world might take from you. With Me you are free to be you. The real you. The you honesty called to at the very beginning of this journey. The you whose core is in alignment with My truth. The you who doesn't fear imperfections or rejections, because grace has covered those in the loveliest of ways."

Lysa: "Rejection never has the final say. Rejection may be a delay or distraction or even a devastation for a season. But it's never a final destination. I'm destined for a love that can't ever be diminished, tarnished, shaken, or taken. With You, Jesus, I'm forever safe. I'm forever accepted."[46]

God calls me, and He calls you, to something more, something new. Let's not settle for the status quo. God has great plans for us in the future, and His next plan could begin unfolding tomorrow. Look for changes. Be observant of the connections God creates to help you walk into the new things ahead.

> Do not call to mind the former things,
> Or ponder things of the past.
> Behold, I will do something new,
> Now it will spring forth;
> Will you not be aware of it?
> I will even make a roadway in the wilderness,
> Rivers in the desert. (Isaiah 43:18–19)

As we move forward in our walk of freedom, we need to remember who we are in Christ. In chapter 13, we learned that our true identity—the real person we are—comes from knowing the One who created us, the One who knew us before anyone else.[47]

God gives us value and worth as a person. We don't need to try to prove our worth. He gives us a personal mission that He has perfectly designed us to fulfill.

Remember my fourth-grade field-day fiasco from chapter 5? Here is a review of the last part of my story:

> The third runner sprinted toward me, extending the baton toward my open hand. As I groped for it, waves of reality battered my mind. *The other teams are ahead. I can't run fast enough. I'm going to finish last.*
>
> The girls yelled, "Run, Gail, run!" Fear froze my fragile heart. *I can't do this.*

I whipped around in the opposite direction. Still holding on to the baton, I raced off the track and darted into the crowd. . . .

If only I'd realized that my classmates' opinions didn't matter. I simply needed to stay in the race and run the best I could.

God isn't looking for perfection. He's not watching for our toes to cross the finish line first. His desire for us is that we experience the race.

I've rewritten the end of my story: "I grasp the baton and start racing toward the finish line. I'm thoroughly enjoying the thrill of living out His calling as I run this race called life."

It's your turn to reach for the baton from the last runner and continue the race toward your finish line. God will run beside you.

Dr. Saltz says:

> Becoming real happens when we accept ourselves in our totality—the good, the bad, and the ugly, the strengths and the weaknesses. Becoming real doesn't happen overnight, nor is it possible without some effort, but when it happens, we experience a freedom unimagined. When we become real, we are able to have the exquisite connection to our lives and loved ones that can only come when we choose to stop pursuing the pain-avoidance filters that also keep out life's pleasure, meaning, and joy.[48]

Dr. Lawrence says, "God has a new identity for you where you will be at your best, fully alive and filled with joy. You will become what you have always longed to be."

Because of my personal relationship with God—who fills me with love, acceptance, value, and worth—I had the courage to begin to reveal the real person I was inside. He can fill you with this same courage.

Supported by your heavenly Father and your relationship with Him, you can surrender your fear of rejection to Him. He will give you courage to stand up from your hidden places and say yes to His invitation to walk freedom's path with Him.

On that path you will become the person our loving Creator meant you to be all along. You can embrace the present and look forward to your future with joy and anticipation as you watch Him unfold His perfect plan for you.

> "For I know the plans that I have for you," declares
> the Lord, "plans for welfare and not for calamity
> to give you a future and a hope." (Jeremiah 29:11)

Lord Jesus, thank You for never giving up on me. Even though I was afraid to come out of hiding and face the unknown, I'm anticipating my future with joy and security because my hand is in Yours. Thank You that You will continue revealing the loving plans You created for me before I was born.

Reflection Questions

Chapter 14: Anticipating the Future

1. What kinds of thoughts enter your mind when you consider stepping into something new—some unfamiliar arena with unknown elements?

2. How might saying yes to something new and trusting God for what lies ahead lessen the power that fear of rejection has over you? Give a possible example.

3. Describe a situation in which you made a decision to say yes or no. Give the reasons for your answer.

4. If you have a personal relationship with God, in what ways has your relationship increased your confidence?

5. Once you know your identity in God and you become aware of the passion and desire God has placed inside you to help others, you will have a foundation for discovering your personal mission. Capture any thoughts you have about your possible mission. How do you think knowing your mission will affect your anticipation of the future? How might it help you decide whether to say yes or no to a new challenge?

6. Paul Richardson says that to taste freedom we must make a life habit of letting go. What have you let go of? Does anything still hinder your freedom to surrender to God's will for you?

7. What has helped you set your mind on the Spirit instead of on your human effort?

8. What changes in your life have helped you live a more authentic and real life? Describe some of your experiences. You may want to record these in the Journal Your Journey section or on your computer or mobile device.

Chapter 15

Living in Freedom

In God's strength, people who struggle with the fear of rejection can walk out of their self-made prisons and taste the freedom that will allow them to become who God made them to be.

I used to be in prison, living in captivity, unaware of my isolation.

God helped me break strongholds of the enemy one by one so I could walk away from my bondage. When I tasted freedom for the first time in my life, I wondered if it would last.

It has. For more than twenty years, God has expanded my borders of freedom in His way and His timing.

The power of the fear of rejection used to rule my life. No one knew, because I hid behind my wall, kept my mask in place, presented a good picture of myself, and tried to be perfect—all to receive people's love and acceptance.

My parents didn't give me the love and acceptance I longed for as a child. God wanted to give me both of these gifts—and so much more—free of charge and without stipulations. All I needed to do was reach out and receive those gifts and accept His offer of a personal relationship with Him. When I did, I obtained free access to Him through prayer.

God reminded me of a conversation we had many years ago while I was working on a writing deadline. Unrelated to my writing project, I had struggled with the question, "Who am I?" I decided to ask Him, and this is what He told me: *You are a woman who loves to work with words. I didn't create you so you could look good or impress others; I created you to glorify Me, fulfill My purpose, and bring pleasure to Me.*

His words ministered to me deeply because they confirmed my identity and my calling. I live in the open spaces of freedom now, and the real me—the one who lives out her identity in God—has a chance to blossom because His unchanging love melted my fear.

When we began our journey together, I presented this description by Dr. Saltz:

> Being real means experiencing life's gifts to their fullest. It means being authentic, strong, rooted. It means that along with the pains of loss, we get to experience the joys of closeness, connection, and intimacy. When we're real, we're no longer like tumbleweeds blown around where the wind blows. We have the strength, the stamina, the courage, the power, and the freedom to go where we want to go. Being real means we can tolerate life's discomforts and ambiguities because we are strong enough to embrace the good and the bad, the black, white, and grays of most situations. When we accept this truth, we will become like trees with deep roots, strong and capable and able to weather whatever comes our way. Being real means experiencing the full spectrum of human emotions.[49]

In this book you have met many people who fought the fear of rejection most of their lives. They lived in captivity, believing there was no hope for them. They felt destined to live as permanent prisoners.

Many of them learned how to break strongholds—deep ruts that led them nowhere—through the power of God. Slowly they began to taste freedom because they had courage to show people their authentic selves, which they had been unwilling to reveal in the past.

John Morgan says,

> We were created in God's image to represent Him to people. Like a blanket, fear covers over the image of God in us. If we hide under the cover of fear, we hide ourselves from the very things we were created to do and be. God understands that we have a tendency to be fearful people, so He clothes us with courage and gifts us with grace to come out from under the cover of fear. Then we can boldly face the interactions we encounter every day and obey the call to love others.
>
> Fear of negative reactions from other people, an inordinate need to be loved and accepted, the desire to maintain the status quo and not make waves—these are all based in a desire to gain security from people. These fears of man constantly attempt to pull us from a place of trust and joy. But real security doesn't come from people; it only comes from our relationship with God.[50]

Our personal relationship with God and our willingness to let the Holy Spirit direct our lives is the foundation for rising above our fear of rejection. Without Him, we are left to our own resources, which are powerless to protect us from the rigors of daily living and the hurtful actions and words of others. By following Him and trusting in His power and guidance in our daily lives, we can taste new freedom to live the abundant life He died to give us.

We will continue to pass through seasons. Some may be full of joy, making it easy to stay on the path of freedom. Other seasons may bring disappointment, health concerns for ourselves or family members, unexpected changes in our jobs, etc., that pull our eyes away from God's promises.

These are the realities of life. Every day, in various circumstances, we have to make choices about how we will speak, act, and live. When that old fear of rejection whispers in your ear, telling you to hide, recognize the deception. Tear down the lie by declaring you believe in God. Reach out and embrace God's truth, which overcomes everything that is designed to delay, deter, and discourage you on your journey of freedom.

> Therefore there is now no condemnation for those who are in Christ Jesus. For the law of the Spirit of life in Christ Jesus has set you free from the law of sin and of death. (Romans 8:1–2)

> It was for freedom that Christ set us free; therefore keep standing firm and do not be subject again to a yoke of slavery. (Galatians 5:1)

Whenever we give in to our fear rather than trust God, we must be sensitive to the conviction of the Holy Spirit. This is God's way of helping us become aware of our sin so we can repent, receive His forgiveness, and walk in freedom again.

Pastor LaGrone says:

> Conviction is the internalized voice of God, affirming our worth, gently calling us to a life better than our own impulses and offering us a chance to change . . .

> Condemnation is a voice that says: you will never change. One is the voice of God. The other is never, ever the voice of God.[51]

Our old internal stories may tell us we are unworthy and will never change. These are stories of condemnation. The stories God wants to write in our hearts are all about grace and forgiveness. He says we are worthy to receive His power to change. Listen to these new stories that will build you up and increase your joy. They are based on the truth of who you are in Christ.

We can live in open spaces, surrounded by freedom and courage to show people what is inside us. The more we let people see the real us, the more we show the result of God's power in us.

Dr. Saltz says we will acquire five important gifts when we begin to live a real life:

- Authenticity
  When you no longer have to build a buffer between who you fear you are and what you present to the world, you experience a tremendous freedom. . . . Authenticity is knowing who we are today and acting from that understanding.
- Personal Freedom
  When we know ourselves for who we are, we feel secure and are less inhibited about trying new and different things. . . . Trying new things is incredibly exhilarating.

- True Strength
  When we stop guarding ourselves, we get personal freedom—freedom in relationships, freedom in taking risks, freedom in pursuing difficult things in life even though we might fail.
- Self-acceptance
  Acceptance allows us to choose our battles and decide how to handle what we're given. When we accept ourselves for who we are, we widen the channel through which strength, creativity, and intimacy flow.
- Intimacy
  If you aren't really yourself with another person, there is only so much intimacy you can have. When you are less critical of yourself and your loved ones, it creates trust and closeness that are the cornerstones of intimacy.[52]

We have been learning how to rise above the fear of rejection. This has not been an easy journey involving simple steps. It's been hard work. Yet when we embraced the possibility of what our lives could be, we became willing to let God's power help us step out of our prisons and break our strongholds. We began to taste freedom to live authentic lives.

> But now, thus says the Lord, your Creator . . . and He who formed you, . . . "Do not fear, for I have redeemed you; I have called you by name; you are Mine!" (Isaiah 43:1)

God knew you would struggle with the fear of rejection. Yet here you are, walking with new confidence and anticipating the future God has designed for you.

By recognizing and acknowledging your fear and relying on God's power to overcome it, you stepped into a life of freedom. Because you gave God permission to change your life from the inside out, you are no longer the prisoner you were before.

As others compare the fearful person you used to be with the person who now has courage to let others know who they are inside, they will recognize how God has transformed you.

Your transformed life is a story God wants to tell the world through you. Your story reveals His power and glory and shows that He created you as a unique design with both strengths and weaknesses.

Your story is God's story. When someone asks, "Will the real person please stand up?" you can rise above your fear of rejection and say, "Here I am."

Do not call to mind the former things,
Or ponder things of the past.
Behold, I will do something new,
Now it will spring forth;
Will you not be aware of it?
I will even make a roadway in the wilderness,
Rivers in the desert. (Isaiah 43:18–19)

Father God, I'll never be able to thank You enough for liberating me from bondage. Now I am walking in the land of freedom. Convict me whenever I stray from Your path so I can continue walking unhindered on my new journey. You have transformed my life. I want others to know the real me, who came alive because of You. Amen.

Reflection Questions

Chapter 15: Living in Freedom

1. Our personal relationship with God and our willingness to let the Holy Spirit direct our lives is the foundation for rising above our fear of rejection. As we continually allow the Holy Spirit to control our lives, our foundation will remain strong. Page 164 contains an explanation of how to live a life directed by the Holy Spirit.[53] On that page, you will see three circles that represent three kinds of lives. Which circle represents your life?

2. If the third circle represents your life right now because you are in control of your life rather than the Holy Spirit, you can apply the principle of Spiritual Breathing through confessing and surrendering (page 165). Each time you realize you are in control of your life, confess your sin and surrender the control so you will be able to live a Spirit-directed life again.

3. Celebrate your journey that allowed you to recognize the reasons you were living in captivity, to break strongholds that kept you in bondage, and to taste freedom that gives you increased confidence to let others know the real you. Walking in this new freedom will be a progressive journey of becoming the person God designed you to be. Take some time to trace your experiences of rising above your fear of rejection and record them in the Journal Your Journey section (pages 160–162) or on your computer or mobile device. The following questions, which relate to the three sections in this book, may help guide your thinking.

Living in Captivity

   a. When did you first became aware you were in captivity?

   b. In what ways did you hide?

   c. What strategy or strategies did you use to protect yourself emotionally from people?

Breaking Strongholds

   d. How do you think your fear of rejection evolved? Family, personal experiences, etc. Describe some details.

   e. What experiences have you had in "tearing down the lies" that were pasted on the walls of your prison?

   f. Describe your progress in "taking every thought captive to Christ" so you can live in the truth.
(See 2 Corinthians 10:5.)

   g. Describe your greatest victory in breaking a stronghold and walking out of your prison.

   h. What other strongholds did God help you break through His power?

Tasting Freedom

   i. In what ways did claiming the truth about your identity give you courage to step onto the path of freedom?

   j. Describe some of your new experiences since choosing to walk on God's path of freedom.

   k. What Bible verses give you the most confidence to keep believing the truth rather than lies?

   l. Have you discovered a new thought process that helps you stay focused on God instead of yourself as you walk on the path of freedom?

   m. What has been your greatest joy since God set you free?

JOURNAL YOUR JOURNEY

(Question 3 of the Reflection Questions for chapter 15 includes suggestions you may find helpful as you record the discoveries you have made.)

Living in Captivity

_____

_____

_____

_____

_____

_____

_____

_____

_____

_____

_____

_____

_____

_____

_____

_____

_____

_____

_____

JOURNAL YOUR JOURNEY

Breaking Strongholds

_____

_____

_____

_____

_____

_____

_____

_____

_____

_____

_____

_____

_____

_____

_____

_____

_____

_____

_____

_____

_____

_____

_____

JOURNAL YOUR JOURNEY

Tasting Freedom

WILL THE REAL PERSON PLEASE STAND UP?

Embrace the Source

Embrace the Source

The following illustration explains more about the Holy Spirit. When you accepted Christ as your Savior by faith, His Holy Spirit came to live in you and direct your life (moving from circle 1 to circle 2 in the diagram below). He became the foundation, the center of your life (circle 2). By faith, you can continually choose to allow the Holy Spirit to control and direct your life. This is often called being filled with, controlled by, or directed by the Holy Spirit.

When you choose to let the Holy Spirit fill, or direct, your life, then your life supernaturally reflects Christ. You begin to bear spiritual fruit—the characteristics of the One who is filling or directing your life. Those characteristics, mentioned in Galatians 5:22–23, are love, joy, peace, patience, kindness, goodness, faithfulness, gentleness and self-control.

Exhibiting these characteristics, or responses, in various situations is not a result of trying to be good or working harder to be loving or patient, etc. These responses are a result of being filled with God's Spirit, the result of His character being lived out through you.

We cannot experience intimacy with God and enjoy all He has for us if we fail to depend on His Spirit. Even though you have Christ in your life, you can choose to depend on yourself to direct or control your own life at any time (circle 3). When you choose to go your own way apart from God, this is what God in His Word calls sin. (This moves you from circle 2 to circle 3.) As soon as you recognize you have sinned (i.e. quit trusting God to meet your needs), you can by faith choose to realign yourself with Christ and allow the Holy Spirit to direct your life again. (You move from circle 3 back to circle 2.)

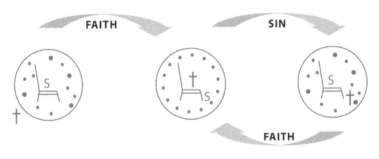

A life directed by Self
Before receiving Christ

A life directed by the Holy Spirit
After receiving Christ

A life directed by Self
After receiving Christ

Journal Your Journey

Choosing to be filled (directed/controlled) with the Holy Spirit is a constant opportunity, not a one-time decision. Every time you realize that you have chosen to go your own way (sin) and are living through your own power (circle 3), you can confess your sin (agree with God that you have gone your own way) and then surrender the control and direction of your life back to Christ (circle 2). This process has been referred to as Spiritual Breathing, or walking in the Spirit. It is a moment-by-moment life style. It is learning to depend upon the Holy Spirit for His abundant resources as a way of life.

Spiritual breathing, like physical breathing, involves exhaling and inhaling. You confess (exhale) and surrender (inhale). In this way you can experience ongoing dependence on the Holy Spirit and open communication and relationship with the Lord.

SPIRITUAL BREATHING

EXHALE	INHALE
Confess your sin the moment you become aware of it.	Surrender control of your life to Christ, and rely on the Holy Spirit to fill you according to
Confess your sin acording to 1 John 1:9 and Hebrews 10:1–25	His command—Ephesians 5:18 His promise—1 John 5:14–15
RECOGNIZE YOUR SIN Areas where you have chosen to go your own way apart from God.	**SURRENDER YOUR WILL** Surrender control of your life to Christ.
AGREE WITH GOD Be specific about your sin. Agree with God about it and be willing to turn from that sin.	**RELY UPON THE HOLY SPIRIT** Rely upon the Holy Spirit to fill you with God's presence and power by faith.
THANK HIM FOR HIS FORGIVENESS Believe that God has forgiven you because He promises to if you ask. Thank Him and then act in alignment with His forgiveness.	
Confession requires repentance— a change of attitude and action.	*Surrender brings reconnection with the Holy Spirit.*

Endnotes

Introduction

[1] Gail Saltz, MD, *Becoming Real: Defeating the Stories We Tell Ourselves That Hold Us Back* (New York: The Berkley Publishing Group, published by Penguin Group, 2004), 3.

Chapter 1

[2] Quote often attributed to Henri Jozef Machiel Nouwen, (1932–1996), original source unknown.

[3] "How to Overcome the Fear of Rejection and Regain Your Self-Confidence," Adam Sicinski, accessed August 29, 2017, http://blog.iqmatrix.com/fear-of-rejection.

[4] Saltz, *Becoming Real*, 4–5.

[5] Ibid., 39.

[6] Sicinski, "How to Overcome the Fear of Rejection." accessed August 29, 2017, http://blog.iqmatrix.com/fear-of-rejection.

Chapter 2

[7] Taken from *A Certain Risk: Living Your Faith at the Edge* by Paul Richardson, Copyright © by Paul Richardson. Used by permission of Zondervan. www.zondervan.com.

[8] Ibid., 160.

[9] Beth Moore, *Breaking Free: Discover the Victory of Total Surrender* (Nashville: B&H Publishing Group, 2000), 1–2.

[10] John Morgan with Joel Balin, *War on Fear* (Lake Mary: Creation House, 2016), 51–52.

Chapter 3

[11] "The Impostor Phenomenon: Recent Research Findings Regarding Dynamics, Personality and Family Patterns and Their Implications for Treatment," Psychotherapy Volume 30/Fall 1993/Number 3, referenced at paulineroseclance.com/pdf/-Langford.pdf.

[12] Cambridge University Press, *The Cambridge Academic Content Dictionary* (New York: Cambridge University Press, 2009), 698.

Chapter 4

[13] "Feeling like a fraud," Dr. Christian Jarrett, https://thepsychologist.bps.org.uk/volume-23/edition-5/feeling-fraud, May 2010.

[14] "Learning How to Deal With the Impostor Syndrome," Carl Richards, accessed August 23, 2017, http://www.nytimes.com/2015/10/26/your-money/learning-to-deal-with-the-impostor-syndrome.html?_r=0 Oct. 26, 2015.

[15] "The 4 Simple Truths Imposter Syndrome is Hiding From You," Erica Moss, accessed August 23, 2017, https://blog.trello.com/4-truths-of-impostor-syndrome.

[16] "Feeling like a fraud," Valerie Young, quote cited by Dr. Christian Jarrett, https://thepsychologist.bps.org.uk/volume-23/edition-5/feeling-fraud, May 2010.

Chapter 5

[17] Martin M. Antony, PhD and Richard P. Swinson, MD, *When Perfect Isn't Good Enough* (Oakland, CA: New Harbinger Publications, 2009), 8.

[18] Julia Cameron, *The Artist's Way* (New York: Jeremy P. Tarcher/Putman, 1992), 120.

[19] Saltz, *Becoming Real*, 17.

Chapter 6

[20] Morgan, *War on Fear*, 24.

[21] Moore, *Breaking Free*, 233, 236, 238–239.

Chapter 7

[22] Dee Henderson, *Taken* (Grand Rapids: Bethany House Publishers, 278.

Chapter 8

[23] Kim Anthony is the author of *Unfavorable Odds* and also a staff member of Cru/Campus Crusade for Christ, where she serves with her husband in the Athletes in Action ministry. Her opening words as emcee of Cru's biennial US Staff Conference are used with permission.

[24] Richardson, *A Certain Risk*, 186–187.

Chapter 9

[25] For more information about *The Significant Woman* life-coaching discipleship course, visit www.TheSignificantWoman.com.

[26] Edward T. Welch, *When People Are Big and God Is Small* (Phillipsburg: Presbyterian and Reformed Publishing Company, 1997), 44–47, 49.

[27] Sarah Young, *Jesus Calling: Enjoying Peace in His Presence* (Nashville: Thomas Nelson, 2013), 339.

[28] Adapted from the Spiritual Breathing diagram on page 49 of *The Significant Woman* discipleship course, copyright 2007, 2011 by The Significance Project and Campus Crusade for Christ, Inc. (www.TheSignificantWoman.com). Used by permission of The Significance Project, Campus Crusade for Christ, Inc., (CCCI) and Bright Media Foundation (BMF).

[29] Dr. Joseph Langford and Dr. Pauline Rose Clance, "The Impostor Phenomenon: Recent Research Findings Regarding

Dynamics, Personality and Family Patterns and Their Implications for Treatment," *Psychotherapy* 30, no. 3, referenced at paulineroseclance.com/pdf/-Langford.pdf.

[30] Robert McGee, *Search for Significance* (Nashville: W Publishing Group, 2003), 59.

Chapter 10

[31] Brené Brown, PhD, LMSW, *The Gifts of Imperfection: Let Go of Who You Think You're Supposed to Be and Embrace Who You Are* (Minnesota: Hazelden Publishing, 2010), 23.

Chapter 11

[32] Brown, *The Gifts of Imperfection*, 123.

Chapter 12

[33] "Everest Climber's Mountaintop Experience," The 700 Club, accessed May 10, 2018, http://www1.cbn.com/700club/everest-climbers-mountaintop-experience. See also: http://www1.cbn.com/video/everest-climbers-mountaintop-experience.

[34] "When Loving is Not Easy," Jo Lodevico Lee, accessed May 10, 2018, http://www.familywiseasia.com/when-loving-is-not-easy/.

[35] Based on 1 Peter 5:8.

[36] Lysa TerKeurst, *Uninvited: Living Loved When You Feel Less Than, Left Out, and Lonely* (Nashville: Nelson Books, 2016), 129.

Chapter 13

[37] Beth Moore, *Here and Now . . . There and Then* (Houston: Living Proof Ministries, 2009), stated during Session Two of the DVD study guide.

[38] See Genesis 9:8–17.

[39] David and Caron Loveless, *Nothing to Prove* (Orlando: Live True Publishing, 2016), 14.

[40] Jessica LaGrone, *Namesake: When God Rewrites Your Story* (Nashville: Abingdon Press, 2013), 204.

[41] "Praying the Names and Attributes of God," Navigators, accessed May 2018, https://www.navigators.org/resource/praying-names-attributes-god/.

[42] TerKeurst, *Uninvited*, 17–18.

Chapter 14

[43] Learn more about Campus Crusade for Christ/Cru at www.cru.org.

[44] Richardson, *A Certain Risk*, 177–179.

[45] Based on Matthew 19:26.

[46] TerKeurst, *Uninvited*, 208.

[47] Adapted from quote by LaGrone, *Namesake*, 204.

[48] Saltz, *Becoming Real*, 16.

Chapter 15

[49] Saltz, *Becoming Real*, 3.

[50] Morgan, *War on Fear*, 62.

[51] LaGrone, *Namesake*, 197–198.

[52] Saltz, *Becoming Real*, 229–233.

[53] Taken from page 48 of *The Significant Woman* discipleship course, copyrighted in 2007, 2011 by The Significance Project and Campus Crusade for Christ, Inc. (www.TheSignificantWoman.com.) Used by permission of The Significance Project, Campus Crusade for Christ, Inc., (CCCI) and Bright Media Foundation (BMF).

Recommended Resources

Gail Saltz, MD, *Becoming Real: Defeating the Stories We Tell Ourselves That Hold Us Back*

Brené Brown, PhD, LMSW, *The Gifts of Imperfection: Let Go of Who You Think You're Supposed to Be and Embrace Who You Are*

Beth Moore, *Breaking Free: Discover the Victory of Total Surrender*

> The following chapters are especially helpful in identifying and breaking strongholds:
>> Chapter 40: Tearing Down the High Places
>> Chapter 41: Deprogramming and Reprogramming
>> Chapter 42: Taking Thoughts Captive

The following website includes thirty descriptions of God's attributes and leads you through thirty days of prayer as a way to know God better: https://www.navigators.org/resource/praying-names-attributes-god/

The Significant Woman life-coaching discipleship course for women
> This small-group course helps women become more intimately connected with God, realize their identity in Him, and discover His calling, which will enable them to live a life of significance.

WILL THE REAL PERSON PLEASE STAND UP?

More information about this course and how you can begin your own group is available at www.TheSignificantWoman.com.

The following products, produced by The Significance Project, are part of *The Significant Woman* course. They can be viewed and ordered through www.TheSignificantWoman.com.

> *The Significant Woman* Participant Book
> *The Significant Woman* Facilitator Guide
> *Beginning Your Journey of Significance* booklet
> *Living a Life of Significance* booklet

Man of Impact life-coaching discipleship course for men
This small-group course uses biblical principles and life-coaching tools to help men learn to live with purpose and significance, empowered by God.

The following products, produced by The Significance Project, are part of the *Man of Impact* course. They can be viewed and ordered through www.cru.org/store.

> *Man of Impact* book
> *Can you Know God?* booklet
> *Living Empowered by God* booklet

About the Author

Gail Porter is an award-winning author. Her book, *Life Through Loss: Facing Your Pain, Finding Your Purpose,* has touched the lives of many who watched their loved ones suffer and were then left behind. Gail can identify with their sorrow because she has endured cascading losses in her own family. She helps readers face the inevitable grieving season and find courage to take the next step toward new life. One couple, having read Gail's book shortly after losing their nineteen-year-old daughter, said this: "Because you showed us how you processed your grief, we were able to walk through our own journey." *Life Through Loss* is available on Amazon.com as a softcover book or e-book.

Gail also co-authored two resources for women: *The Significant Woman* life-coaching discipleship course and the *SOARING* life-coaching evangelistic course, designed to help Christian women reach their non-Christian friends. Both books have been translated into multiple languages in other countries. For more information and to order books for a group study, visit www.TheSignificant-Woman.com

Her newest book, *Will the Real Person Please Stand Up? Rising above the Fear of Rejection,* contains chapter-end questions that make this book easy to use in a small-group setting. By using the special *Journal Your Journey* section at the back of the book, readers can preserve their notes and discoveries throughout the three parts of this journey: Living in Captivity, Breaking Strongholds, and Tasting Freedom. Books can be ordered from Redemption Press at redemption-press.com. Also available on Amazon.com and Barnes andNoble.com.

Gail welcomes your feedback and questions.

Gail speaks at women's conferences, at church and community events, in corporate settings, and in group gatherings. To request her to speak, you may contact her through her website or email. Some of her topics are Discovering Life through Loss, Releasing the Fear of Rejection, Walking in Freedom, Living Out Your True Identity, Finding Your Purpose, Building Bridges of Harmony and Growing in Christ.

Blog: www.liveabovefear.wordpress.com
Facebook: www.facebook.com/gail.porter.731
Website: www.gailporterauthor.com
Email: contact@gailporterauthor.com

Find her latest book on the Redemption Press website:
https://www.redemption-press.com/featured-authors/gail-porter/

Order Information

REDEMPTION
P R E S S

To order additional copies of this book, please visit
www.redemption-press.com.
Also available on Amazon.com and BarnesandNoble.com
Or by calling toll-free 1-844-2REDEEM.

CPSIA information can be obtained
at www.ICGtesting.com
Printed in the USA
FFHW021928210819
54431342-60136FF